Crossing The Street

By

Richard Bergkessel

A story of the Catholic Priesthood lived in a fresh manner

References Re: S. Dolorette
Pages 133, 134, 136-138, 139
141, 142, 159, 194, 196, 198, 199

Crossing The Street

Special Acknowledgements

Fr. Richard Rohr offers the line in his book **On the Threshold of Transformation**, "We need to fail, to fall, to jump in the central mystery of our own existence or we'll have no way of finding our true path." **Crossing the Street** is my attempt to share the life of a priest, dispensed and "returned to the lay state", who continues with his family to minister within the Catholic community. As a couple and a family, the Bergkessels travel across the country through four dioceses, **Crossing the Street**. It was a fantastic adventure to grow in wisdom, age, and grace with many others, in many places. Through his journal, Richard offers us the Spiritual Journey of a "Priest forever" in the ever-renewing Church.

Richard Bergkessel

Preface

THE PLAIN DEALER

CLEVELAND.COM

(Reprinted by Permission)
By Darrell Holland
Religion Editor

A former priest who resigned from his ministry in the Cleveland Catholic Diocese in January last year to get married wants to serve the Roman Catholic Church again as a priest.

Ricchard A. Bergkessel of North Olmsted, a social worker for the Center for Human Services here, said his marriage to a former nun has not diminished his desire to work as a minister in the church.

He is a member of the Chicago-group, Corps of Reserve Priests United for Service (CORPUS) which includes 427 of the 7,000 former priests in the United States.

Bergkessel told The Plain Dealer in an interview this week he endorses the service's the desire if members to be priests.

He said he has mninisterial skills which could serve the needs of people, and that the church could determine where he could best work.

Bergkessell, 34, born and reared in Garfield Heights, was graduated from St. Mary Seminary and was ordained in 1967.

He left the priesthood early in 1974 and was married last November. His wife, Charlotte, teaches in a parochial school.

In the seven years he was a priest, Bergkessel was associate pastor of St. Hillary Church, Fairlawn, and St. John Bosco Church, Parma Heights. His last assignment was an associate director exlof St. Joseph Christian Life Center, Cleveland.

Bergkessel said he is a member in good standing of the Catholic Church, and that he attends St. Richard Church in North Olmsted, where he works on the adult education committee and the worship commission.

According to the church doctrine, once a person becomes a priest, he is always a priest.

Technically, Bergkessel explained, he is still a priest who has resigned from his ministerial career with the permission of Rome.

Bergkessel said he has informed Bishop William M. Cosgrove, auxiliary bishop of the diocese, of his desire to work in the church either as a priest or a deacon at least part time.

He said Bishop Cosgrove relayed the message to Bishop James A. Hickey, head of the diocese. The diocese said the situation had been discussed, but that it had no comment.

He emphasized neither he nor the service intend to protest demonstrate or issue ultimatums that former priests be readmitted to priesthood.

Rather, he said, they envision contact with married prriests and concerned bishops and church officials to attempt to get former priests an opportunity to work either as priests or deacons.

Bergkessel said the diaconate, the first and lowest ministerial order in the Catholic Church, could provide a starting place where former priests could work, at least on a part-time basis.

Deacons do not celebrate the mass, hear confession or anoint the sick. But, they can perform baptisms and marriages.

Ordination as a deacon is the first step toward priesthood though there are permanent deacons, and some of them are married.

Before Bergkessel and other married priests could be readmitted to priesthood, the church would to change its law on celibacy, a move which Bergkessel conceded he did not expect to happen very soon.

But, he said, the church could open the door to the diaconate rather quickly to former priests who are now married.

Asked why he wanted to ret-enter the ministry, Bergkessel said, "I have talents, abilities, and insights, all God-given, that blossomed when I was an active priest.

"Despite the fact that I am married, I am interested in being a minister, in sharing myself with persons who need help. I have been called and trained to be a priest."

He said neither he nor his wife regret that they left their religious vocations to marry.

He said he was not trying to cause trouble for the church, nor to contest the authority of the church or its bishops. "I just want to fulfill my priesthood," he said.

He expressed fearr that news coverage of his desire to work as a priest again would make the public regard him as a trouble maker.

The service has maintained that married ex-priests who desire to have a ministry should be permitted to do so because of the shortage of priests.

The group has asked that former priests be considered much like reserve units in the armed forces who could be called upon when the church needs them.

Table of Contents

3

Chapter One

Setting the Stage

It was early spring of 1974. I was a social worker at the Center for Human Services. I had just transitioned out of the active priesthood of the Catholic Diocese of Cleveland, Ohio, and I was driving toward downtown Cleveland on a crisp spring morning. I caught sight of a young man about to cross Prospect Avenue. As I watched, he measured out the proper time to venture forward to make his way through the traffic to the other side. I was struck at that moment of a parallel in my life. The maneuvering involved in navigating an intersection and planning the steps I had to take in changing my lifestyle were so similar. When crossing the street, there is a purpose involved. Anticipating and avoiding obstacles and problems on one side of the street weighs on one's mind while on the other side of the street, a smaller crowd gathers, another destination is beckoning, another friend awaits. I watched the simple act of someone making his way from one side to another and I thought of how my new life presented a challenge to be met, a new vision of hope to attain, and a new life or adventure to pursue.

No one could know why that young man on Prospect Avenue crossed the street that morning; the reason *I* crossed the street back then, in 1974, is why I am sharing my story today. Just as that young man crossing Prospect Avenue found drivers who were sympathetic and helpful by pausing for him, so I will share the many circumstances, persons and graces of the Lord that enabled me to find my way and fulfill my mission in life.

From the very beginnings of my venture crossing the street in the mid-70s, to the time we settled as a family in Yuma, Arizona in the early 80s, the spiritual motivations I encountered became a foundation to my growth in faith. These inspired me personally, and have become central to our family. As you read this, I hope you will be inspired too.

I journaled much of my central life happenings and these entries captured amidst many, many days, weeks, and years of me and my wife, Charlotte, building a structure of our spiritual journey. Later, as we welcomed our three children, the day-to-day growth of us all lends much to that same journey. When I first began writing, my focus was on the central fifteen-year swath of time in our family life. Upon reading what I initially wrote, a good friend of mine of 16 years described our story as one of lone rangers that had been dropped from the sky in mid-adulthood with no previous life lived. Moved by this, I decided at that time to shape the story of my life into a context of childhood, youth, and young adulthood. To understand me and our story, you must read how I became the person you are reading about. And, you will learn the reasoning behind my decisions, and what enabled Char and me to raise our family in a 'fishbowl" atmosphere. The stories I had grown up listening to from my very early childhood as well as my own memories of growing up are 'stand out' events and coming of age building blocks of my lofty ideals of serving others in The Catholic Church.

The Beginning: Richard and Charlotte

In 1941, Charlotte and I were among the 2.7 million babies born in the United States. Charlotte was born on August 8, and I was born on October 2. She entered a large family as number seven of what would be a family of eight children. I, however, came on the scene as child number three with age differences of 13 and 14 years from my brothers, Eugene and Ernest. In effect, I was an only child and the start of my parents' second family.

I remember one story of Eugene as he left home to go into the army. My mother was crying as he went to the train. I was not close to my brothers because the lengthy age difference between me and them, but, because my mother was crying, I also began to cry. The depot was a very huge, impressive hall that even today, has an awesome effect on newcomers, visitors, and local commuters. I'm told that I screamed as loudly as I could in the large, echoing halls.

Mom and I bonded early in my pre-school and early childhood education. I was her companion as she went to her women's club meetings and to church events. Once I can remember, in the early morning hours, I heard my Mom and Dad begin to argue about something. It so affected me that I stepped between them and began hitting my Dad because I could see he upset my Mom.

My father, being a very hard working, disciplined man, rarely showed his feelings of tenderness toward the family. Yet his care was understood to be present. They also were faithful, religious people. My mother was always the involved woman in parish affairs, often in leadership roles. My father was not a joiner, and as a quiet man, did not get involved in organizations or even many activities. In fact, I can remember a small photo taken of me, running from my father. That photo has always been the only memory of he and I at play together in my early years.

I attended St. Therese School in Garfield Heights, Ohio, through grade eight. The record shows that I missed about 45 days of school in kindergarten and Grade One.

I did not like school! With that in mind, I found every excuse to stay home, leave early, and be uncooperative. I was so difficult, at one point, the teacher drove me home after school to have a meeting with my mother. That was the worst instance I can remember in kindergarten. And, in first grade, I recall standing in the front of the room pounding on the nun's heavy habit crying that I wanted to go home.

This bundle of insecurity settled down in the second grade after I had my tonsils taken out and First Communion preparation began. Plus, it helped tremendously that my teacher was the greatest thing since sliced bread! As I continued at St. Therese, I thrived on my growing ability to mature and become a leader. In Grade Four, I became an altar boy and by Grade Six, I was elected president of the altar boys. What an honor! I remember being so proud to have been chosen by boys older than myself! My brothers were both married by this time and My dad and I often drove to visit them on summer evenings. These were prized moments; I savored being with him. I began to see his steel-worker image breaking down.

During my middle grade years, I began having thoughts of wanting to be a priest. The three priests at the parish served my idealism of the significance of the priesthood. As soon as this interest was known by the priests and religious sisters, they were quick to protect and promote my thinking. In 1953, our family built a brand-new house and at the beginning of my seventh-grade year, we moved into our new home, two houses directly beside our parish. Because I lived practically on top of the church, I became available for more opportunities to be involved. Before the move, we lived more than a mile away and my Mom did not drive. My relationship with the parish and its priests grew stronger over time.

As children do, I emulated the adults around me. I can remember pretending to be a priest, saying mass, and imagining myself in that role. As the seventh grade began, I decided that I would like to go to the seminary for high school. I entered Borromeo Seminary in September of 1955, thanks to a young man who became a priest and began discussing the idea with the school leadership and then, with my parents. I had always assumed I would attend one of the local high schools, yet, when this offer arrived and we went to visit the school for a tour, I was deeply impressed. My parents were supportive and my Dad, in his typical quiet way, agreed to pay for my tuition. The experience was very much like going off to college, however at age 13, instead of 18.

This is where the beginnings of the idealism of the priesthood met the realism of hard work and study that soundly challenged me. These years brought a growing maturity as well as the normal adolescent interests in girls. I had a growing interest in greater freedom and my self-identification was quickly taking shape. The school was set up to emulate another school in Baltimore called St. Charles, also for young men. There were three buildings, each with three dormitory rooms for sleeping 20 guys in each room.

Through these high school years, as an attempt of self-identification, I thought much about leaving. Yet, I put a halt to that inclination when I was asked to take a role in a class theatrical production. Soon, I began to look ahead to my senior year when I would become a dorm prefect and have the leadership of younger men. The school's faculty and officials were increasingly taking note of my own competency.

School work was very difficult for me. I made it through but it was a challenge, a challenge I've always analyzed because of the stiff competition. There were *really* smart men, that seemed as though they did not have any work to do. The learning just came to them. At one juncture, as a junior in high school, we were taking four languages--English, Latin, French, and Greek. School started at 8:30 am. And, all morning, we worked on language after language and then lunch. Sometimes it was just plain hard to the bone. It was during this time that I thought seriously about pulling back and saying, "I can't do this." There were eight or ten more years ahead and I had only been through two. All I could think of was: Is it always going to be this way?

Once, during this time, in a Latin class where we were seated in alphabetical order, the teacher called on me. I had an answer but, sadly, it was far from the right answer. I was sitting next to the windows, the kind that tilt out in two levels, and there were blinds pulled closed with cords many feet long. When I gave my incorrect answer, the priest grabbed the cord and wrapped it around my neck saying, "Are you nuts? Wrong answer!"

While I didn't think much about it then, later as an adult I considered the significance of that action and the meaning of abuse. That moment stuck with me and has remained with me until now as I share this. During high school, many young men left school, withdrawing from the program. For me, I found myself holding on to this fact: No matter if it's hard or not, you must press on to get to that end goal.

Sometimes our teachers were old men. In fact, many were either close to retirement or should have already been retired.

The educational system was classic European which means you didn't learn a language to be able to speak it or to read it. You were required to read in different languages but it was all European style of memorizing paragraphs in French and Greek. It was a lot to take in.

Throughout high school, I missed my home life. I often questioned, "How am I going to do this?" Despite many guys and young kids around your building and dormitory, you still really did not know anyone. There were a lot of rules. Everybody is in the same boat as a freshman so you keep moving forward, talk to guys, and adjust. When It was frightening, you could go in the corner and cry a little bit.

When I finished my freshman year, another guy in the parish, Len Duritsky, talked about the possibility of going to the seminary and I encouraged him. His family was close to a different assistant priest who also encouraged him. He decided to go and do what he had to do and his uncle, a priest in Pennsylvania, paid for everything. We went to school together and were close, although you wouldn't have known it at school. We just didn't associate with one another but when we would come home on summer vacation, we were inseparable. Together, we both had learned how to drive and the priests would give us their cars to use. What a thrill those days were!

In my sophomore year, my health became an issue. Another kid and I, at the very same time and the very same day, were diagnosed with rheumatic fever. At that time, I discovered that I had a heart murmur. It was funny for me to tell someone that I spent three weeks in the hospital at such a young age. I knew that I would either be put behind from missing so much school, or tossed out because I was so far behind and I couldn't make it up.

Consequently, after two long hospital stays with rheumatic fever there was consideration of my dismissal. Yet, for some reason, my doctor took a great interest in me and my case. He was deeply concerned about my seminary status.

Eventually, he wrote a letter to the school leadership on my behalf and because of him and his compelling letter, I was permitted to continue in the seminary and I graduated along with the rest of my class.

When college began, it brought many more academic challenges. The work load at times was overwhelming and my own self-doubt in my ability to make the grade was persistent. The addition of my ongoing health concerns was an ever-present sense of discouragement. I found myself losing my dream of priesthood among a maze of school routines and countless regulations. I maintained my resolve; only my closest confidantes knew of these struggles. Soon, a priest advisor helped me determine that I definitely wanted to be a priest. There would be no further vacillation or questioning. I made up my mind that I would leave only if I were asked.

My mother died one week before I graduated. After she was gone, I came to see my Dad as a very warm and feeling person who needed me very much. I accepted this and even found it to be of further help in maturing. I entered St. Mary Seminary Graduate Theology School in the fall of 1963 with a high level of determination. I was convicted and believed deeply that these last years of preparation for the priesthood would be years where I would grow in knowledge and ability.

That is exactly what they proved to be. My studies no longer overwhelmed me and I found I could handle them along with the highly responsible duties of sacristan. I grew in self-acceptance and in my interest in ministry. I was ordained a priest in May 1967.

This is where my story, **Crossing the Street**, begins

Chapter Two

In Your Will is My Peace

My first assignment as a young, newly ordained priest was in Akron, Ohio – St. Hilary Parish. I was the only associate with a wonderful pastor. In his quiet way, he allowed me to move and work with a great deal of freedom. I was very excited and had many ideas borne from my newfound abilities. It was not long before the parishioners began to accept me and I found quick success in this parish. Vatican II Church was still new and its changes brought me to the re-structuring of parish life. I was gaining a sense of self confidence that was growing by leaps and bounds. The people of the parish began to rely on me to help them with multiple needs and through this work, I soon grew very close to many in the parish. Having not experienced much interaction with women in a largely men's environment, I found contact with women on a personal level to be new. I was becoming more aware though, of the need that every human experiences, that is, to be loved and to love personally.

Before long, my rewarding years at St. Hilary would end and I was offered and accepted an assignment of a very large suburban parish in the Cleveland area – St. John Bosco. Unfortunately for me, I found this a difficult adjustment because of its rigid structure. The pastor there, unlike my first assignment, wished very much to be in control.

My Expanding Gifts

My vision of priestly ministry began to expand during that one year of service at John Bosco. I saw that I had a very definite ability to touch people's lives in a deep and valuable way. For example, I was invited to give several Sister retreats. Through these experiences, I felt a need to change ministry and soon, I was offered an opportunity that matched my burgeoning skills. In July of 1973, I was named Associate Director of the Diocesan Retreat House.

During my five years of active ministry, I came to believe in the paradigm shift of the married priesthood. I became an advocate for it as I could not see that marriage would be a hindrance to a person serving a parish community. Along with this changing interest in ministry, I saw my personal spirituality grow. I had found a renewed zeal in prayer. Another shift that impacted my life during these formative times in ministry was another drawing movement in my heart. In 1971 and 1972 I came to be in close relationship with a sister.

Charlotte and Richard: The Beginning

Charlotte was serving in a suburb about 20 miles away from me. She was a principal of a small school of 250-300 students in the Akron area Catholic School system. There were four nuns who divided up the leadership. Char was 29 years old and had been teaching a while though she was apprehensive at first taking the principal position so soon. The group of sisters she was with pledged to help her and they did. This small group was very close and remained close for many years.

The pastor was a real stickler. He wasn't a mean man, but was the type that was always watching everyone to be sure they were following all rules and regulations. One morning as they were having breakfast at the convent, he arrived with a directive: "I don't care who, but I want two of you to go to the Cursillo that's coming up in a couple weeks."

A Cursillo is a process somewhat like a retreat with an origin in Spain. It begins on a Thursday evening and ends on Sunday. They are usually held at a parish with a gymnasium or a hall to house everyone. Cots were set up for sleeping and a large meeting room is where the talks and discussions took place. Charlotte and another nun decided to volunteer. It was held at the parish where I was assigned. I was the Spiritual Director for the Cursillo. Among the participants were 40 women, another priest and me. I first met Charlotte there, it was the first weekend of May 1971, and her name was Georgine, Sister Georgine. A party person at heart, she was the kind of person who everyone could count on to get things going. It was not unusual for her to be at the center of everything, and all the women would circle around her. Her bubbly personality grabbed people's attention; everyone was attracted to her.

Throughout the weekend, Charlotte always had something to say or to do. The experience was very interactive, rather than simply a lecture. It was an opportunity for people to be trained and become prepared, with presentations, witnesses, and testimony. The two priests offered the teaching portion. When it ended, Char and I did not make plans to see one another again, nor did I ever hear anything about her. Then one day, just before school started in late August.

My pastor approached me to tell me he had been asked to give a talk about the relationship between pastors and school principals. He was not interested in doing the talk and told me I knew as much as he did as I had been at the parish a few years by then. With that, he said, "You do this talk and tell them I sent you because I am not feeling well."

The pastor had had a heart attack and subsequent heart surgery. And when the day for the talk arrived, I went alone and introduced myself.

Since Charlotte was a principal, she was there to participate. The two of us talked a bit and at the end of the day, we had dinner. There was another Cursillo happening in October at another parish. There is a part of the retreat that is meant to bring people together to understand that they are being supported by many others. I went to that event Saturday evening and Char and I got together outside in a garage where a large community of people would serenade those going from the hall to church. A prayer time would then follow in the church. In the meantime, we were waiting in the garage outside of the church talking about my upcoming birthday. I would be turning 30 years old. Charlotte smiled and asked me if I was having a party. I told her I'd be lucky if anyone even remembered my birthday. The next thing I knew, she was saying, "Oh, NO!" Charlotte immediately started talking quickly telling me she would speak to Carolyn, who was the cook, and ran the convent house. Carolyn was caught up in Charlotte's infectious plans and agreed quickly.

The next day, Charlotte called me and said, "Yea, Come! Carolyn's going to have a dinner and is baking a cake for you. We are having a party for you." It ended up that I also had a surprise party at the rectory with about 30 people to celebrate my birthday.

That year, I had a double party--two cakes. Then, in October, a group of sisters decided to go to an out of town retreat, away from the Akron area. Friday Night/Saturday, and asked if I wanted to join them. I said I was interested but that I would need to return for the weekend parish work. When I said I didn't know where the location was, they informed me that I would be driving there.

When I arrived at the convent meeting place, I learned that Charlotte lined me up as a driver but she was my only passenger.

We had an hour or so alone to talk for the first time ever. We both chattered about ourselves and all sorts of things.

Life went on after that and soon, another entire school year came and went. By the end of the year, Charlotte and I had become close. We never talked about leaving ministries but a person would have had to be a dummy to not see it happening. The end of the 71-72 school year would be the end of her teaching there as the school closed. Charlotte was teaching in the Pittsburgh Diocese for most of the next school year, yet we both continued to grow even closer. As 1972 drew to a close, I invited her to get together over Christmas vacation.

And, in 1973, we finalized our decision to leave the ministry. I wrote about it to her, and she to me and our letters crossed in the mail. We decided to go to an extended retreat, individually. She went to the suburb of Detroit and I went to the city of Detroit. Both retreats were led by or directed by Jesuit Priests and the spiritual director of hers, was an older man. She left at Christmas in 1973, I left in the middle of January 1974.

We had already talked to her parents and the sister she was closest to. I, too, had told my brothers and my dad. The most difficult was sharing our decision and plans with my Dad. We told him together. I'm glad she was with me. Just by being there, she softened the blow of it. My father was very confused by the whole thing. He had many questions: How can this be? Are you doing the right thing? Are you allowed to do this? In January, my stepmother died, and shortly after, in March of that year, my Dad died. I got permission to preside at her Funeral, but I did not consider it when my Dad passed.

Life changing moments continued to call our journey in the direction of His Will. We shared our decision with our religious superiors, our families, friends, and the various communities that we were a part of at the time. The process of dispensations took about one year. We married on November 7, 1974 in our living room. Father Joseph Schell, S.J. witnessed our vow exchange.

In July of 1976 we moved to North Canton, Ohio. I began employment with St. Paul Parish as Director of Religious Education. This became a very challenging yet graced time in our lives. We returned to Church ministry, but with a real twist – I was not the reverend priest, but a lay person with a long title.

My Reflections from the Retreat in Detroit
Leaving the Ministry

In the city of Detroit at the Jesuit house of Formation, I spent ten days in a privately-directed Ignatian Retreat guided by Howard Gray, S.J. There I was given a series of Scripture passages to reflect on and to journal. I share some of these passages and reflections here.

> *"Keep me, O God, for in you I take refuge...my heart is glad and my soul rejoices, my body too, abides in confidence: . . .*
>
> *You will show me the path to life, fullness of joys in your presence, the delights at your right hand forever." {Ps. 16}*

I realize that all – even Char and I coming together – came from the Lord. In this, I find a power beyond measure. This is a moment of confidence. My life is non-life without God. He is personally very close to me.

> *"Let integrity and uprightness preserve me, because I wait for you, O Lord." {Ps.25}*

The challenge before me is to recognize and accept the fact that there is a difference between accepting the Presence of God in words of belief and trust, and the full act off allowing, welcoming and following that Presence as my life's chief guiding principle.

> *"The man . . . asked to come with him, but he sent him away with the words, 'Go back home and recount all that God has done for you. The man went all through the town making public what Jesus had done for him." {Luke 8:28-29}*

The actions of my life, my display and testimony of faith, my giving or holding back are a tremendous influence on others. I am placed in a key position: much has been given to me and even more is called from me. Jesus does the calling. He supports as is necessary. Moving elsewhere is not important. Positions of prominence and stature are secondary. The significance of Jesus' remarks to me is that He wishes me to be in the place where I am as His servant, His witness, His holiness. Here is the level of life examination that I must act upon:

"If you repent, so that I restore you, in my presence you shall stand: And I will make you toward this people a solid wall of brass." {Jer.15: 19, 20a}

Purification of heart and life goes on, the hardness of our living response is softened as the healing power and presence of the Lord operates. I need to place myself in the wide-open space of acceptance – easy or difficult, pleasant or distasteful.

David's Sin – "David, however, remained in Jerusalem." {2 Sam 11:1 – 12:25}

The easy way is to stop growing. When this occurs, a style of living echoes a spirit of dishonesty. The irreverence of the gift offered, and gift refused is likened to knowing our Father and using Him or not knowing the Father and refusing to learn of Him. I see myself as hanging back, taking and accepting but not giving enough.

The dishonesty that haunts me, in that I am writing the lines of my way but not noting the directions of His way.

> *"Coming within sight of the city, he wept over it and said: 'If only you had known the path to peace this day: but you have completely lost it from view! . . .*
>
> *they will wipe you out, you and your children within your walls, and leave not a stone on a stone within you, because you failed to recognize the time of your visitations.'" {Luke 20:41-44}*

I am the city that the lord has placed amid his world and people. He wills that I be for many – a source of relief, safety, hope and shelter. I question why Jesus is weeping over me.

The startling challenge is to examine my reasons for action, my motives of thought and the goals of my life. A tempo arises from the sounds of my heart. It is harsh.

A basic selfishness in my living and ministering must be written out of the rhythm. As this change occurs, the city of my life will brighten in the darkness – again being a leader of the way.

> *"Your attitude must be that of Christ: though he was . . .. God, he did not deem equality with God something to be grasped at. . .. he emptied himself . . .. he was of human estate. . .humbled himself. . . accepting even death. Because of this, God exalted him and bestowed on him the name. . . so that every knee must bend. .*

.and every tongue proclaim Jesus Christ is Lord!"
{Phil. 2:5-11}

Jesus is the meaning for life, relationship, friendship, and love. The sacrificing of all for the sake of proclaiming "Jesus is Lord" is the Christ quality necessary for successful ministry. The compelling thought strikes: the resolutions and decisions I make and live by cannot be complete, honest, and acceptable without prayerfully meeting Jesus as Lord in my life.

> *"The crowds asked him, (John the Baptizer) 'What ought we to do?' In reply he said, 'let the man with two coats give to him who has none. . .Eat nothing over and above your fixed amount. . . Don't falsely accuse anyone.' He will baptize you in the Holy Spirit and in fire." {Luke 3:10-16}*

The basic components of my life must involve service and care for others, marked with a high degree of honesty and respect. I need to possess an exciting, growing, ever purifying similarity to Jesus as Savior.

> *"Whoever wishes to be my follower must deny his very self, take up his cross each day, and follow in my steps. What profit does he show who gains the whole world and destroys himself in the process?". {Luke 9:23, 25}*

Jesus is not one who just uses words. He weighs each phrase and idea so that a value and purpose is shared with those who listen. His words are not only to be heard but to be listened to, reflected upon, and digested as a part of life – our very being.

In His remarks on discipleship Jesus offered me words of hardness, challenge and yet of strength. The call to deny self is an invitation to know, value and love myself in an ever-deepening manner. The weight of my daily cross is the yoke of other's burdens embraced by me.

When striving to accomplish these facets of the Lord's call, I realize that I am solidly in His path, following Him to the glory and praise of the Father. Here is my strength to go on.

Chapter Three

Growth in Our Parish Ministry

I have always looked upon the years from 1989 to 1992 as the central part of our story. In these days, weeks, months and years, I longed to capture our growth in parish ministry through journaling, written reflections, and prose. While I continued my work at St. Francis, Charlotte began to be more deeply involved in Religious Education. The Church, in general, likened this work to a never-ending love of learning more about one's Christian faith and Char was on board with her focus of CCD or as she promoted it as Continuing Christian Development. The Pastor and Associate Pastor recommended me as pastoral administrator with particular attention to adult areas of formation.

St. Francis joined a small number of other parishes in the Diocese of Tucson, in adopting the pastoral spiritual renewal process called RENEW! The key element to this movement was for individuals and couples to meet in a small faith sharing group for six or seven weeks twice a year for four years. Materials were prepared by the national office in outlines, sharing guides, and sensitive scripture passages. As I was appointed the parish staff director to implement this new process, I worked closely with the lay director, Herb, to roll this out for the 300-400 parish participants.

SUNDAY, JANUARY 1, 1989

Friendship has been a resounding note for me today.

Char and Donna, my brothers, Len and me-- our family. The calmness of the day presents strong hopes for the new year.

May Char and I bond ever more deeply and securely through all the non-imagined events of the months and days ahead. As Brian, Lynn and Dave continue to mature, may our care and love of them be ever individual and to their maturing benefit.

Lord, keep me and us within the friendship of your love. You have chosen this place and this time for me to be a part of your mysterious plan. May I be attentive to your call, grace and will for me. Make me truly gentle – strong in tribulation constant in prayer.

During this time, Char and I moved seamlessly into parish leadership ministry. It felt completely natural as the general parish also transitioned into its renewal process. We traveled to Tucson for training at a diocesan conference related to local parish renewal. I was inspired and excited as we drove together to learn new thoughts and ideas, and then discuss them among other church leaders. I saw these as sacred moments.

Char and I were fortunate to be entering a time where she recognized the beauty of who we were and what we were blessed to do. We shared the same visions, hopes, and intentions, though our approaches varied, we continued to keep these shared ideals central. We would eventually learn how deeply challenging this seemingly simple commitment would be. Much of the early months of 1989 were taken up with my attempt to juggle any number of ministry efforts as well as a maturing family of five.

As our plans unfolded, Char found herself tied-up in the stress of ministry and the unfortunate demands of health issues.

It is a struggle to live a fast-paced life, often steeped in chaos. I learned so much about myself during these days. The many questions children lob at adults often reached my ears creating a conflict within me.

I found that in the busy every day, I often viewed their questions as a bother only to remember later that they were touching me, caring for me and I needed only to acknowledge them. Another lesson in self-awareness was that I found I behaved differently in public than among my family. I prayed for the ability to reach out to my children, appreciate them, and understand that my impact on them as people was for their entire lives, and not just for the moment.

TUESDAY, JANUARY 31, 1989

"Church business" as Char and I continue to share and reflect on our work – we see that our prime work is to listen. To seek anything else is not truly responding to your call and guidance. To glory in this is always a temptation. It is nice to hear about 'running things", "power position".

Keep before us (me) that sense of mission – sent, by You, to gift as I (we) have been gifted.

Jesus, I give all to You!

The season of Lent for '89 was filled with a wonderful spirit of the Lord's Word to us, his abiding presence, and the great mission He sends us to fulfill.

The more I worked on my focus of my own children, I continued to learn new insights. For example, I was surprised to discover that our children, who I believed held their friendships in the highest regard, were, in fact, most moved by being with us at Church Sunday morning or anything else that Char and I were doing. Whether we were racing or looking for four-leafed clovers in the park, playing basketball or getting things ready at church, they loved these moments most. I grew to see that as parents, we make life so difficult when it's the simple things that truly matter. Brian especially liked the idea that I was involved as a leader and as an "in charge" person. He thought that was a big deal. When he was younger, I would approach the dais to read the scripture on Sunday. I'd look down and Brian would be standing right next to me. The people in the choir up in the front, were tickled and thought it was the cutest thing. Our children wove their way into our work.

I went to Yuma with the conviction that if the pastor wanted me to, I would learn Spanish. With a parish of about 1800 families and nearly 500 of those families being Spanish-speaking, the church assigned a separate director who handled all kinds of activities and kept them together. There were Spanish Masses and from time to time, we tried some bilingual Masses to bring everybody together. There were good aspects to this and some not so good, yet no matter what, the Spanish-speaking Masses always outdid us in music--always very joyful and loud. Char was a very upbeat person. Even amidst all the sickness she endured, she was so very strong and worked very hard to beat her illnesses. While in Yuma, she ended up in the hospital a half dozen times with asthmatic attacks. An optimist, she was always one that looked ahead and knew that there were always possibilities on the horizon.

These days generated many doubts and fears as Char suffered physical problems and our finances suffered right along through. We continue to form as a pastoral team, grow spiritually as a couple – married, ministering, parenting and facing all manner of challenges. The spring and early summer found Char interviewing for the position of director of the children and youth aspect of formation. I continued to grow in my role of parish administrator as the position also grew and further developed.

SUNDAY, APRIL 9, 1989

A very typical Sunday! The obvious harmony between Char and me is witnessed by our exchange in the adult class.

Picking up loose ends touched the day -- shopping, tax doing, going with kids for ice cream. If I were in Char's shoes with asthma, I would be very lonely, isolated in the family. The question of why would hang over me. How hard, what a journey she has made to become so resigned to her lot. More positively, the power of Jesus' Spirit is at work in her. She accepts the power and is enabled to be the best she is capable of being.

Thank you, Lord, for Char in my midst. May I learn and be conscious of you as I experience her grace-filled instrumentality.

Later that year, in the summer, Char gave me a method to pray and journal, to discover more fully the working of the Lord in my life. First, I write as if Jesus were writing to me a letter of encouragement; Then, I write back to Him. I started this approach in the long, hot July days when time creeps by ever so slowly.

TUESDAY, JULY 11, 1989

Dear Dick,

You have stayed close to me -- I've remained close to you! The more that I beckon is not to be all you're working for, but rather just being there and letting me move in, through and around you. As you keep your eyes and ears open, I am here. Those around you most often exemplify my presence. I am touching your heart in these early morning moments.

WEDNESDAY, JULY 12, 1989

Jesus, I love you but, rather putting aside all hindrances of following and responding to you, I place more in my path. At first, I call this being selfish, dumb, stupid and ugly. I am struck that I am, weak, but constantly called to let you be who you are to be in my life – the power! Over me and caring for me. How wide the gap between knowing and being and doing! Jesus, you bring all the situations of my life to this point – My challenge is to examine the purpose! Constantly!!

The Bergkessel Children and Ministry

Just as Brian loved to be with me during Mass, all our children understood that my role and Char's role made us leaders in the church community.

They saw us as important, the "bosses" in charge and they liked that their parents were so involved. Their friends came over for overnighters or for a weekend, and I'd take a whole bunch of them over to the church.

We would set up chairs on Saturday afternoon for Sunday Mass in the hall for the overflow crowd. Eventually, we started a family Mass at 8:30 am on Sunday mornings. The experience was a bit different, a little bit looser, and the kids were involved a lot more. Our kids began to know the routine and enjoyed being in the know on it and they got right to it.

Once a little girl--a friend of Lynn's-- walked over with us to the hall and she said to Lynn, "Does your Dad own all of this?" Her father was the owner of a newspaper in Arizona. Yuma Daily Sun. I smiled thinking how her Dad owns things, she just expected that I owned it all too. It was a sense of satisfaction that they were always very proud of that fact. Of course, sometimes I didn't like the consequences of being in charge on the community stage. Once, David got in a fight when he was about 9 years old. I don't know how much fighting a 9-year-old could do but he fought with a kid who was a little bit bigger than he and two to three years older. This happened outside the door before Sunday school classes started. There were a lot of people around. I thought to myself, "Oh my gosh, what in the world? Everybody knows he's my child and he's fighting with some other kid outside of Sunday School." The other fellow was a serial trouble-maker. Who knows what 9-year-olds fight about but I broke it up and sent them to their classrooms. When we got back home, after everything was finished, David was very contrite about the whole thing. (Even though he tried to say that the other kid started it).

Yuma was a growing community and our children had lots of friends. They played all kinds of city sports programs. Despite our positions in the church community, we did not expect them to be the 'perfect' children. Brian, our oldest boy, chose on his own to be an altar boy and was very good at it. He liked the pastor.

David did not want to serve as altar boy yet the pastor always called him King David, and still refers to him as that today. David chuckles even today when I share with him after a phone conversation with Richard, that he asks about "King David".

Burn-Out and the Struggles of Ministry and Family

SUNDAY, AUGUST 27, 1989

Another day of blessings – involvements, RCIA, family, play, relaxation, CODA at night.

Jesus, you lead me along paths that go in only good directions. Some paths are rocky, some are narrow, and some are smooth with ease of movement. The past few days have been beautiful paths with ease of movement. The tendency is to think that the ax will fall. Yet, with true knowledge of you, I understand that in all situations you are with me. Thus, my outlook needs to be continually adjusted.

Jesus, may I look to you always, in all ways, and with all whom I meet.

MONDAY, SEPTEMBER 11, 1989

Dear Dick,

I inspire, I teach, I prompt, I grace, I care about you and how you do your life, ministry, family, all things.

Be open to me – listen with heart and mind. Be free in the expectation of my gifts. I will guide you in all things. Use the insights, knowledge, and direction of others to know yourself! Please sense the utter value of my care and your attention.

I love you, Dick.

TUESDAY, SEPEMBER 12, 1989

Dear Jesus,

I know all that you are and do for me. Yet, as the feelings come to play, I fail. I am not as sensitive as I want to be. I place my homily thoughts in your hands. May the words you desire to be said, be used by me as your instrument. How easy to become enmeshed and codependent. Always why!? The things that trigger – Char's bad feelings – I grab. Her anger at others – I aim at me. I latch on to others – I must stand independent!

Jesus, I thank you.

Most of the next year, 1990, became a see-saw of ministry events, goals and short-falls that wore on me emotionally, physically and spiritually. Perhaps the rumors began to squeak out that our time of ministry at St. Francis was losing its luster! Very early in my time as a priest in parish work, I decided that six to seven years was about the proper life cycle to stay in a parish community.

In the waning days of 1990 our family took on more than just a church position, but became somewhat of a social centerpiece. We hosted a gala Thanksgiving Day dinner with about 10 guests beyond our family. It was a pot-luck affair with me providing the "stuffing" that had become talked about due to my bragging and Char's praise.

There's a bit of history to this! In 1982, our first year in Yuma, the Church weekly newsletter ran an ad for families to welcome a couple of Marines for Thanksgiving dinner. We did that and two young men came to our home. I prepared the meal from a recipe I found in SUNSET magazine for a one dish turkey meal. The key dish was the stuffing--even our children liked it-- and that is how our stuffing tradition began!

At the 1990 gathering there were two marines, their spouses and families; two Religious Sisters, from the school staff, and several of our friends. I remember I struggled with focusing on the preparation. The meal was a blur and I recalled being unable to really savor the experience and compared this to how life was working at that point. I was often exhausted: Prepare; Get Ready; Race; Rush; and Worry. My prayers were for balance at that time.

MONDAY, DECEMBER 3, 1990

Well, here I am – a long weekend of kids sick, newspaper delivery, shopping, running, being hyper, tired, work, -- busy there too. Holding on to so much – tightly so that things break loose! Control kills! All odds up to my codependency and compulsiveness.

I feel refreshed this A.M.! It is Advent, Christmas is 22 days ahead. Perhaps a difference will happen in me. Jesus, I enter this pilgrimage with joy – allow me the grace to recognize that the events, works and movements of this day bring me to walk more closely with you.

"We are the clay,

You are the potter

We are all the work of your hands"

I don't want to cut short your work!

TUESDAY, DECEMBER 4, 1990

Working with David was a special time yesterday. He really was wrapped in to what I was doing. For me, I felt lifted that he joined me, that I could welcome him into my world. He was and is special. How I need to communicate that very often to him.

Last evening's work was long and tiring, but of great benefit. The realization I had a couple of years ago about drinking my work as sweet tasting rather than bitter is valuable to hold to now.

Jesus, allow the moments of today to pass as sacred. Enable me to savor them.

WEDNESDAY, DECEMBER 5, 1990

"I don't want the ram in the thicket, I want you Jesus; call to me. You want me here, not there!

How busy I make myself in the morning. I enmesh myself in each child's life. Can I long endure? I have so many wants and roads to take!

Tonight's Reconciliation Service! Jesus enable me to piece together all the details. May I budget out my day in a reasonable manner

Chapter Four

The Day to Day

In my grand scheme of life, I lump together the years 1991, 92 and 93. I named this segment of life <u>The Grand Canyon</u> and anytime I think of it, I think of "Murphy's Law." As we move ahead, what can go wrong, not work, or fail to happen, does! Much like a soap opera, the days during these years come and go in a rather slow-motion style. Not much happens on any given day or even at any given event, but there is always a subtle stirring of life just below the surface. In so many respects the early months of '91 ran along with only a rare bump in the road.

MONDAY, MARCH 4,1991

Brian remains a source of tension with his illnesses. Where have all his friends gone! Is he obsessing on golf! Jesus, I place him in your hands. Hold him tight. Give Char the wisdom to see and seek him out to discover where he is.

I wondered during these days of where I would go next after Yuma. I struggled with negativity and often turned my thoughts inward. Char's health suffered and her asthma restricted her breathing. Restlessness crept into my days and I found myself questioning my role at the church. I had ideas of ways to improve our mission, yet found I was keeping them to myself. Asserting myself became more and more difficult and there were frequent times I found my prayers were to accept the Lord's will for both of us and our family.

And, at the same time, I began to think about where our future lies and what was next for us.

TUESDAY, MARCH 12, 1991

Like shit, <u>conversion</u> happens! Unlike shit, it is gift – whole and complete. But, again, like shit it is often messy, grabbing us and taking control of us. It is burdensome, and always attracts our attention.

In very subtle, gentle ways conversion is happening! I didn't make it, I am letting it. It is a call to answer and urge to accept, a challenge to feel good (about). It is discovery while shocking, it is health in sickness. It is light in a tunnel. It isn't the end, it is a reawakened beginning.

"Jesus, keep Serving it up!" Amen   Thank you Yes!!!

WEDNESDAY, MARCH 13, 1991

A friend is coming! I guess I hold feelings of real joy that I can speak to a friend on an equal plane, about non-threatening things in a man's manner. Yet, Russ is a third party – rooted in Church – a wounded healer. Thank you, Lord!

Needed to Share

> *1) Mass – Presider – Worship thing.*
> *2) Job – Administrative Assistant*
> *3) Future?*

As I sit here and think – these are very <u>big</u> matters.

WEDNESDAY, MARCH 20, 1991

I'm in a <u>really</u> searching, wondering mood and spirit. The turmoil is the lack of peace I feel knowing what it is with Char. I look for, seek, to think through the means to fix and to satisfy, and to clear up and restore peace again. I'm overburdened with the prospect of her dissatisfaction with me, us, the parish, the Church. A real redemption complex.

Touch my mind, soul, my whole person to let go. We have done right. We have responded whole-heartedly. What is left is the task of sharing the vision, the package, and the picture. How to better do this – teach – preach – point the way.

Jesus, may I follow!

THURSDAY, MARCH 21, 1991

The dying of Jude, Fr. Richard's brother comes to mind. How little the value of all the small in life. The values we place are so often really misplaced. Even all the things we must do lose their power, significance and luster. There is a real strong openness to death that gives a freedom – a letting go of for a greater feel, life and hope.

Jesus, give me a day to be more than to do! Guide me to be for others in an accepting and understanding. May I not be consumed by fears but have the experiences of freedom, to share your message message of full life for me and all.

FRIDAY, MARCH 22, 1991

Death reigns! A startling phrase, but so real. One to think about often, to allow it to touch the core of my life. What is important to me today!? Who is important? Why? Momentary grace. Let it sink in.

Jesus, to see the preciousness of health and life is important. I place Char in your hands – hold her, nurture her, give her comfort without pain, let her feel your healing power. In mind and body give her a strong spirit. Why must the physical side of life be so hard on her? It is straining!

THURSDAY, MARCH 28, 1991

Holy Thursday – ordinary and extraordinary. A day like others, but still standing apart.

There must be feelings inside, I'm moody – irritable! Why? At least, I'm recognizing them.

I get caught up in the symbols and ceremonies of the night.

Service	*greed*
Ministry	*hatred*
Care	*denial*
Food	*self-serving*
Nourishment	

Where do I fit in? Every day the test is mine to see where!

Priesthood – a dream to let go of in one style and embrace in a much more demanding manner. What does that mean? If I but allow myself, I discover every day.

The Grand Canyon is Arizona's pride! We look at it, experience it, as our son David and a girlfriend did a few years ago. They went to the bottom and back up. It's a harrowing task! How does my story fit into such an adventure? My daily living involves me in the disciplines of the hike.

TUESDAY, APRIL 2, 1991

Why does there need to be such pain, anguish, suffering in Char's life? It isn't just physical and breathing that torment her. She suffers in mind and heart over so much.

Am I as good as I appear about letting go? Calm and even-keeled – without any turmoil or hurt? <u>Hardly!</u> I say I can live with it. True to some extent! I'm famous for the suffering I do, I don't rock the boat and confront. To me it is never worth it. Yet, now I know that I must get it out. To be sensitive to ways and means is most important. It has to do with my very survival.

FRIDAY, APRIL 5, 1991

The old money worry is creeping over me. We continue the spiral down to deeper depth. I know the only way out is discipline – to be able to say no and do no!

To plan is my challenge. To have others enter in, to be a part of the process. I can't continue to hold on and hold in.

Letting go is a must!

To make lists and plans is a must. To accept slowness. To pray for miracles and surprises is a must.

To discover within myself all that I am capable of being is a must.

Please, Jesus!

Let me only look at parts at a time – not the big picture. It's too overpowering.

MONDAY, APRIL 8, 1991

I never write on the weekend. Sometimes it's a burden – I must work at it during the week. Well!

This AM I'm struck, as I am so often by Char's push – drawing, pushing me out of myself. Not all good or bad! It can be energy growth, or it is merely buckling under. I decide this.

Jesus, I look toward today, as one to be for my family – "self" time, work time, planning time, family time. Give me the self-containment and spine-strength to be in this fashion. I don't feel driven! Guide me. I don't want to be hyper! Calm me. Give me, Lord, the wisdom to discern and a pattern to grow.

TUESDAY, APRIL 9, 1991

Coming to grips yesterday with the finances we are involved with has helped my psyche. As with so much of our lives, this is not going to be easy. A lot of discipline will be needed. My forte has not been this area. I'm too much the pleaser. To take the hard line is to be a winner.

Jesus be my strength in all of this! Grace my day with your touch of calm, peace, hope-giving.

WEDNESDAY, APRIL 10, 1991

Life is sacred! All of it. What a thought. To ask permission is essential before the use of something or someone. Respect the sacredness of myself. To say what I mean and mean what I say is essential also. I am special.

To praise and thank you Lord for Char is so strong in the weaknesses she recognizes. Lift her feelings!

THURSDAY, APRIL 11, 1991

A bright day! The insight of yesterday – Bri's tape: I must call a halt to assuming Char's hurting. At least to the extent I often do. Yet, I feel there is a tight rope between not getting into her hurts and becoming insensitive. Sensitivity isn't one of my strong points to begin with!

Brother Jesus, walk along with me today. Allow me to feel you, sense your word, touch, advice, correction. Enable me to love you as I reach out to others along my path. In the mystery of it all may I see you in them and may they recognize you in me.

Enrich my calmness...

Allow me the ability to be non-lazy as I am wanting to be so often!

FRIDAY, APRIL 12, 1991

I will untie all the strings I put on my love of self and others!

Often at the Canyon, rocks slide, not destroying anything or injuring anyone. It could be the beginning of something reportable.

Such was my experiences as the Church and its culture, tossed about in the same characteristic fashion.

WEDNESDAY, APRIL 17, 1991

Confirmation Day! Bishop contact! What are my feelings! Char sure has hers. I am numb! He cares but can't show it. He is nervous! He is cautious! He is truly an introvert! How does this affect my feelings? I've classified them out! I analyze all, I come out swallowing hard, stuffing much. I say – what difference do I make. He avoids me, doesn't really want any deep conversation or will avoid it if it comes.

I accept some feelings of bitterness. I am, tonight a sort of functionary. I've set up the guides, the lines, the whole very "churchy" stuff. This leaves me with bitterness! Tonight's parade of dignitaries is of poor quality.

You can bet -- Char, as the only one who has been personal to these kids, will be least appreciated.

Another incident occurred as the parish celebrated First Communion Day with the children. By this time at St. Francis, I worked out a very good means that each child would be able to sit with and receive Communion with their family around her/him. It was a beautifully orchestrated celebration of faith and family. As the community was departing, I overheard an older gentleman say how wonderful the Sisters are who work so hard with the children.

The man knew me, I stepped up to him and said, "My wife Charlotte and I are responsible for all of the planning. The nuns did not have a role!" His response with a surprised face, "Oh, Nice work."

FRIDAY, MAY 17, 1991

I start my 10th year with St. Francis. An event! A time marker. I wonder how much I could write if I took the time – to consider beginnings, confidence, make a mark, the pains, the nerves, the pressures, the ideas, hopes, angers – expressed and stuffed, the dreads, the person, the arguments and embarrassments. My journeys with, for, because of; the moves, curves, the strategies. The inspirations of being moved.

Now – how far I have really come. Name, power, yet, to be recognized as very committed to and very bruised by the Church, the parish, the system is of great import.

I'll do my best, knowing my strengths and limits.

A Father and Son Adventure
Looking Back, Looking Ahead

The canyon beckons! As I stand on an edge and look out to the vastness of depth and distance, I am taken back to the place that was home for me, for Char, even for our young family. I begin to desire to know my parents, what is the story of my family – my roots.

In January of 1991, we had been in Yuma for some time. Back then, Yuma had one paper--an afternoon edition.

They delivered on Saturday and Sunday in the morning time. Brian had a paper route delivering it. He enjoyed his work because it made him money; he was big on having spending money. At 13, he was close to his cousin, my brother's daughter who was three years older. They always got along well when they got together. It was around this time that Brian told me he wanted to go to Ohio to visit her in the summer. His idea was to travel to Erie, PA, and meet up with her. He didn't mention me at all; his idea was to go solo. It was then that I had the idea to go along. I approached Char about it, asking her what she thought about me going along for the trip. Brian's idea was to go for an extended visit, about a month.

Char was behind the idea and said they would get along fine on their own. Since I normally had a month's vacation from work each year, I spoke to the pastor about going at the end of June, he said it would be fine. We made our plans, got ourselves together, and left sometime around the end of June.

Brian, a golfer, insisted on taking his golf clubs so that he could golf at least with his uncle, my brother and perhaps with me, too. I didn't take my clubs. Brian and my brother, Ernie, golfed together a couple of times. At that time, my sister-in-law had two adult sons living in Florida who they often visited. That summer, while Brian visited, they traveled to Florida taking Brian, and I stayed behind in Ohio to visit many of the folks that I knew from the experiences I had as a priest in Ohio.

As I left on vacation with Brian, I left behind a somewhat major project. I drove an initiative through the parish staff and the pastor, Fr. Richard, regarding the need for the children and youth religious education program to have a highly visible presence in the school building.

I proposed that a storage room of good size be remodeled into an office/resource center for Char and the C.C.D. program.

THURSDAY, JUNE 20, 1991

Time to travel is near! The days go by. There is much to prepare. There is much to do. I'm calm about it all; I will walk away and leave. Life will go on – I can't meet all the needs. Should I try?

The remodeling work? Turn it over.

MONDAY, JUNE 24, 1991

This is the last day that I'll write here. To travel – journey. To leave behind. To go back to. To savor the past blended with the present. Seeking out our roots to discover new about myself.

Letting go is such a challenge. These things that I'm part of here are so engulfing, that letting go is difficult. Who will answer questions?

In my codependent fashion, I aimed to look at this visit as a mission rather than a vacation. I wanted to delve into my family past and my own more recent past. It was surely a change of pace.

WEDNESDAY, JUNE 26, 1991

A day of travel and being tired gave way to a rather relaxing and nurturing kind of time.

Plane trips and connections were easy. Brian was quiet, very cooperative, mature in acting, especially with Russ!

He was somewhat of a pain as he wanted to rush off in the AM today.

Off we went in a pickup!

Aloneness feelings haven't sunk in yet. Marveling at the outdoor pleasantness that here is judged hot.

It's 7:15 PM in the back yard of some retreat house south east of Erie that J&E are on the Board of Directors. Woodsy, restful, bird-filled. There is a sense of – I've been here before not this place as much as the kind of place – the childhood, youth, before of my life.

I'm beginning to look at this trip as a very extended retreat time. I had to, with difficulty, last night realize that I can't plan all of this out ahead – cover all bases and button it all up! Day by day – one at a time. Don't worry!

A real feeling of jealousy strikes me as I hear of Jan's inheriting from her Mom. Those who have, have more. Why can't our life be a little more plain and less burdensome. Yet, to see this blue-bird at the feeder just now, restores a sense of being gifted and cared for in some very special ways.

THURSDAY, JUNE 27, 1991

This is a day of some emotion, happening, discovery, pain, hope and Thank You, Lord.

Goodbye – hard to set out alone. Typical, but not for long. Caught up in the sharing and lives of Donna, Jack, Jenny and Stacey!

Visiting Dad – surprise – Hedy -- not alone with him as I desired, O.K. He was good – but totally unsure. With you and then not, certainly not the man I had known. Reality was Hedy's as she broke down when leaving.

Boating -- air, land and water. The strong combination of so much to the senses. Beauty in simplicity.

Talking with Char – the afternoon and the evening. Calm and uplifting as I shared about Dad, she yet sits with the burdens of the outcome cannot be done away with. It comes in many shapes and figures. We do the waiting game now.

The setting of this family is <u>"fascinating"</u> to watch – so much is left unsaid when you think all is said and done – a judgement – an observation – a reality.

A new day dawns – Jesus keep me open to the possibilities.

SATURDAY, JUNE 29, 1991

To be touched by people's lives and their issues and then walk away is very difficult. I will talk with two classmates tomorrow and hopefully to see Jim.

MONDAY, JULY 1, 1991

A good visit was had by all! Nick had surprises – a house, accomplishments in work, photography and solid life-outlook

My brother's tightness! Two cars—won't offer one to me. Over-protective of little Richard – the one car is old. Yet, I understand where he is coming from. It's easy to quarterback on Monday morning and see all the errors that others make.

TUESDAY, JULY 2, 1991

It's noon and I've made it to North Canton. Deepest memories come, I walked through Price Park. The same in many ways, but improved – walking path, long and winding past old park area. Pond is the mark of fishing with grandpa, feeding ducks as still goes on swings that sway. Bri for countless hours through infancy, toddlerhood, terrible 3's, and the pole he finally grew to slide down. It's a bank of our early years.

The condo did little and the pine tree house – not much more. Very wooded as the front yard trees are huge. As everywhere I go, so much building is going on!

Again, as elsewhere, I don't even plan on recognizing anyone or they me.

Some thoughts – <u>life</u> was simpler here. That's not to say better or more fulfilling, but simpler. A stage! If we had stayed, perhaps, changes and growth would have occurred too.

Listening to sagas of people's lives, it's neat to walk away.

WEDNESDAY, JULY 3, 1991

I don't have to hold on to other's troubles and experiences. I enjoy giving of myself in all my visiting.

Being alone is really hard for me. Filling the quiet, being still in a quiet room, alone, is almost overwhelming. Why? Typical man!

FRIDAY, JULY 5, 1991

Dinner – a wholesome looking family. Loving and Gentle; accepting these children as truly adults.

Dicks – how much tragedy is a family able to cope with? Death, Cancer and another child, Alcohol of another. Jesus be their felt help – all, children and each.

An evening to remember – The Lettermen! So much of what is happening during these days is a nostalgic trip that comes to the present. 30 years of music and song!

Time to move into a new day – to travel some, meeting again, the new, yet old!

Jesus may the line, "when I become skilled at touching my own spiritual source, I will know it is truly impossible to be alone," energy me to see the mission, that is fully mine!

SUNDAY, JULY 7, 1991

An evening with John Vrana! Hurt, yet learning himself, John is not complete. I walk away again affirmed in where I am.

The Church in the "burbs" is a whole different adventure – not necessarily a discovery of greatness. To me it has been an exercise in the adage – bigger and more is better. To contrast with Russ' situation is enlightening.

What touches me is my own know-how, skill and feeling in church work that doesn't set me afield from the mainstream of life.

MONDAY, JULY 8, 1991

An experience that few have! Sitting with some noteworthy, graying, radical souls – a blend really of thinkers who know their directions--Karg, Kraker, Yohner, Caddy, McCafferty, LaRocka, Russ and me.

It's 10:30 AM and I just went for a one hour woods walk in Metro Park – Rocky River – near where we lived. I haven't seen water yet! Nor a picnic area we may have used. I'm going to drive around and look.

Sweaty – flies and bugs all around my head – from the shampoo, I guess. Prevented reflection. Yet, greenness is great. A whole other dimension of god's creation – interjected with the roar of an airplane – man's creativeness! I experienced the feeling of youthfulness – among these ancient trees and ground, rocks and river beds.

I think about God's plan! Why am I now at this park bench?   It's been such an experience of full discovering for two weeks!

Asked if I miss family – and no was the answer, but then again, not really. There is a growing sacredness for each of that I treasure and miss holding on to.

I sense the need to respect distance, be less caretaking and more self-respectful in the family circle and in the work place.

It's hard for me to be still and enjoy -- need to see, do, accomplish.

Jesus, -- peace I seek, peace I be!

FRIDAY, JULY 12, 1991

A quiet, cloudy and slow-moving AM. I enjoyed golf with Don and two others. Lot of sharing – mostly on Don's part. Not an easy life either! Almost too much – but <u>with help</u>, all that he could handle.

I get nervous, even frightened to think what may lie ahead.

It is really clear that Don's faith and its effect on his life is very strong. Is mine? Where does growth lie for me!

Going into the garden! The discipline called for here needs to be planned and truly worked at. Where is this place for me in my life? The desert of my soul -- for revival. Alone and with others.

THURSDAY, JULY 18, 1991

I sit in the backyard at Donna and Jack's. pleasant – all are asleep. A boating evening – Brian was neat. Youthful daring, fun loving, naturally conversant, and in so many ways, ideal. I really cherish him. Their exchange students stands in contrast. An immature, insecure and manipulating youth – spoiled by having too much. Harsh and probably reading in some reflection of my own.

FRIDAY, JULY 19, 1991

Late in the day, for my writing – 5:30 PM. Brian and I played golf in AM. Poor place – usual score – good for Bri and I. Pretty – much he and I together for PM until Ernie came home.

Shared yesterday with Ernie our money woes! He is super-concerned. Plug the leak! Rebuild! His advice is stop charges – ALL.

Budget certain amounts to areas of constant expense. Get this down as low as possible.

Devote some extra to monthly pay out on highest interest rated items. At least 3 years in a very disciplined plan of action. Maybe 5, depends on our effort.

I've thought about myself over the past few weeks. A more disciplined manner – we joke about so much of what and how I do – but there is truth to it. Cut my breakfasts out and down to two a month with Dick.

SATURDAY, JULY 20, 1991

Late at night! My stomach turns. Jim Stieber committed suicide! Where to turn! Russ has been trying to reach me. Floods of regret! Could have done something differently – Sandy! Where is she?

How are the children.

All else pales in the midst of this.

TUESDAY, JULY 23, 1991

Evening of full day – Golfing with Brian – 27 holes – that's a story. Long walk in Metro-Park – Brecksville.

Continue yesterday by visiting Sandy! The funeral was touching – an opening for tears for me to see this family coming in with a friend – dead. The time was for memories – Ron pointed to hands – Theirs as they become competitors/friends through handball. Jesus holds us in his hands.

Cemetery – touching time as Tom O'D, John V, Ron and I lead the burial prayers. It struck me how much more I feel the feelings of Sandy, Sherri, Debbie, Jim and Steven. Marriage and family do make a difference at a time like this. The reserve of these others showed itself to me.

I visited with Sandy today as she asked me to do so yesterday. A time for listening. She has much to let out! Guilt and courage! They will complement each other. We are still aunt and uncle – Sherri remembers!

As I waited all afternoon for Brian, I was struck to tears about the commitment and closeness Char and I have and must maintain. The preciousness of the moment!

Our vacation draws to a close in peacefulness – real – tragic! Simple.

Tomorrow as I travel, I will write of my learning and resolves.

Little or no eating out! Decide our priorities – where to spend, to save, to be settled. NO WORRY PLAN.

Mode of less pressure to please others as the basis of my doing!

It's all right to be unorthodox! Casual!

BUDGET for Goals - Savings. Security. Travel.

Letter writing: Defining friendships.

My judgements   Doings at home: Priorities!

My Work: Priorities!

I look out the window of the plane – desert.

My heart is here!

The beauty of the plain is as the beauty of green.

Home – the open land for me – where I am free.

I surprised many people and, I'm certain, imposed on some to host me for a day or two. Gratefully, no one acted terribly put out.

With Dad out of the house for a trip across the country, Char, Lynn and David knew how to have a good time and have a good time they did! While in Ohio, I visited, I drove, I met-up with priest classmates, I drove, I stayed at people's homes. And then, I drove some more, and I toured some sights in Cleveland. The time went by quickly. Soon, it was time for me to go to Erie to pick-up Brian. When I finally met up with him, he was bursting with stories about his trip and time with Ernie, Jan and Cathy.

Chapter Five

Changes and Strife

I decided to host a surprise 50th birthday party for Char while traveling in Ohio. To help with the surprise, I planned the celebration for the day before her birthday. Brian and I arrived at home July 29, and to say the least there were problems and issues at the parish. Fortunately, at home, all was in good shape.

SUNDAY, AUGUST 4, 1991

To be firm and act upon my beliefs. Work scope is an area of key importance. Skill development in this area of administration. Say what's on my mind with Richard.

The value of family life! The paying of the price for past looseness in the financial areas. Careful not to get totally pre-occupied. My non-manageability of money is the basis of my need to let go – let God.

Char and I need time for ourselves!!! What kind? When? Let's talk about it.

TUESDAY, AUGUST 6, 1991

Transfiguration – Transformation – To see the Lord in his power and glory – to know that all the unhealthy power of modern destructiveness was initially unleashed today – What have we done! The world being bonded is starting to repair! Then the Gulf War! Are we learning?

The Spider's Web! Catch me, Lord.

May I experience your Glory, not to build, but to harvest for you. May I listen and in so doing, be soil for your seed – love and care, yet strength for others.

May I be gifted today with the insight to be wise!

Thank you, Jesus, for Surprises!

WEDNESDAY, AUGUST 7, 1991

A Party. A Surprise. A stepping-stone of life.

Embrace Char, Jesus. May she feel your touch, love, beauty through those who come tonight. She could use all the goodness and support she is given.

I am becoming pre-occupied with this remodeling project – the school! Here is where the poverty of all lives. We don't have, so we don't do.

The party was a huge surprise for Char. She was lying down for a nap when the guests began to come. In fact, we had a bit of tough time getting her to awaken for the party! A good time was had by all!

THURSDAY, AUGUST 8, 1991

Happy Day! Surprises! Not as dramatic, but as valuable. Fitting into Char's life, it was great. Beginning to laugh!

Jesus, enrich her in these days. Don't let the pains of family, work, health gnaw away at her. May she see you through those who gather around her – last night!

Give courage and the wisdom of clear thinking to those who broke into Char's office – return all and pay for damaged property.

Protect us, Jesus!

Inspire a sense of non-attack, non-abrasiveness on those looking at the budget tonight.

FRIDAY, AUGUST 9, 1991

Explosions yesterday – I'm still reeling. I'm imperfect – I forgot! But I've been accused of wronging! With Yvonne also comes the additional person who will stand against me. The feeling of being opposed is hard for me to hold.

But that may be the issue – I don't have to hold it. I may let go of all and be clear headed enough to speak the truth and stand firm. Even to do and be this, I find myself doing a lot of rehearsing.

The other whole part of this is a slight movement to take charge of my life.

MONDAY, AUGUST 12, 1991

Fridays' day – nightmare! Where do we stand? Does anyone know? Is this a call-challenge to again discover who I am!? I see so many issues and problems that I feel the need to solve – yet, how foolish! Letting go is my greatest need.

The week ahead – Sharon! Another moment to take a stand.

Jesus – give me an even-keel! Firm determined, yet respectful.

Richard – push him to stand up in the counting position.

In the meantime – today – give me the courage to relax – enjoy golf and all else that comes – even prayer workshop.

What unfolds through the next weeks and months is a gigantic effort to remain on the Canyon path and, also, to ward off the dangers of others, friends and foes.

The tensions between myself and lay leaders in the parish came to a head over the parish budget that I proposed. I was leading an effort to advance the position of religious education through the programs of children and youth, young adult and adult formation, with on-going attention on parish spiritual renewal.

The parish council meeting in August,1991, became a pivotal juncture for Char and me to continue to minster here at St. Francis of Assisi! I let the journal tell the story.

WEDNESDAY, AUGUST 14, 1991

Such a tense start to yesterday! The same feelings of anger, wonderment, run-away are all still here. What held on the longest is the "get-away" – move out attitude!

Shaking the dust is such a strong mode that it strikes fear, challenge, and determination into one's heart. I keep saying – why not?

Jesus, I come seeking what you will for me – I look for signs! Is a move for me? Now?

Char – be with her in this day. No matter how much I want so much to be perfect, I find so little that is.

My thoughts now run rampant. Again, giving use to discouragement is ever present.

Jesus be my help!

FRIDAY, AUGUST 16, 1991

Wow, what a day and night!

Confrontation! A feeling doing it! Conquest of self! Becoming "Wild" but what came then was the hate, dislike, built up revenge and anger to be exploded. The wild man is not acceptable! Cut him down – get him. This will not be the end of the story.

My feelings now – the morning after – fear, for myself and for Char – we will be under stronger attack. Anger – how can this be happening when I look to the progress and lives that we touch. Worry, I still want to control – I have not controlled here and I won't have control any longer. A giant First Step!

Jesus, lead me this day.

TUESDAY, AUGUST 20, 1991

The saga continues in the head and in the heart. Some indicators: weight, prayer, expressed anger that is misdirected. All these highlight that all isn't well – I can easily deny.

What strikes this AM – not really focusing through prayer. Always the doing becomes key. Placement in HIS hands! Distractions are so many.

WEDNESDAY, AUGUST 21,1991

I'm not poor – me.

I'm strong. I embrace the dying – the cross – for real! The strength in knowing that no matter what is said and done, the right way needs to be followed. The way of truth! To stand for, with!

Jesus, give me peace! Calm me, I feel like a surging, weaving, upset soul who is terribly afraid of confrontation – more so than I used to be. Enable me to stand and count. You will hold me as long as I give my ability.

THURSDAY, AUGUST 22, 1991

Hopefully a unity of vision will emerge today! The pain of separate-ness and wildness! I feel positive at this moment, You are at work. The cross is still operative. Good is coming. Not win/lose! Win!!!

As Char says – affirm myself through the day. Turn the fear and worry mode into the more normal nervous being ready for a healthy session. To step outside of the issues.

Jesus may this day be of calm preparing – hopeful in every way. May the Spirit be my Excitement.

FRIDAY, AUGUST 23, 1991

I'm still reeling this AM. I'm angry. I'm tired. I feel abused. A lot of negatives were said last night. They were left on the table and the clear impression was left that wrong-doing was done.

I have feelings of being abandoned. There was no expression of confidence expressed by anyone.

Is Frank an innocent by-stander, uncommitted enough to offer any word of support to fellow staff? Sister keeps her veil straight and comes off white-princess "victim."

This AM I'm not sure how long I am able to endure here! I don't have to continue to submit myself to this abuse. Obviously, my gifts are not appreciated. Sharon in her rage mode on 8/15, stated clearly that she and I could no longer work together since she is not trusted by me. That is dead right. I will not be able to provide my talent to the leadership of the council. The process done on their own initiative.

Where does Richard stand in this? What does he expect of her? Does he thrive on being beaten up by her?

Lord Jesus, convict me of where to stand – here – elsewhere – in Church – out of Church! Help me to be open! Clear my head, my heart! The strong negative feelings are healthy now. Place in my path positives that enforce your will!

Someone needs to define to me what is my area of responsibility for the parish budget and its supervision! My sense last night is that Sharon will not let go! I will not "watch-dog" or anything else with her involvement.

SUNDAY, AUGUST 25, 1991

Paying the price!

Making up for what is lacking in the sufferings of Christ! How? What is my burden – I walk with Him.

So much is pouring out. Is there an end? How self-consuming can this become! I'm hating it all. Sure not peace and harmony. I want to fix it all up.

Feel upset! What's that mean? I want to get by all of this. Run away. I want to be distracted – divert.

I can't keep going over and over it all again and again – in my mind, heart, with Char and others. I don't want to deal with it now – maybe later, tomorrow on my terms and time. I'm looking for separation! Health? Wise? I don't know or care at this moment.

MONDAY, AUGUST 26, 1991

How this first day of school has been overshadowed. To go or to stay? Where are the possibilities of change? Jesus, show me! What am I not able to change?

WEDNESDAY, AUGUST 28,1991

Such pulls. To stay put – to go elsewhere – to file bankruptcy – to seek financial counseling – all seems to be question marks. Then in the work-place are the pressures: who's calling? Who's coming up the stairs, is Sharon there, why, what's she doing?

How long, how strong, why us, now, suddenly? Will it end, do I have to end it? Is it all in my mind? Char is a strong influence!

I know I need to create some distance – discover how to move!

Jesus be with me today. Give me some directions, some guidelines. It seems more and more are becoming unmanageable.

THURSDAY, AUGUST 29, 1991

As this day begins, I carry all the tension and imprisonment I felt yesterday. Why such?

Are you telling me something Lord? Is this work here been soured? Is it becoming counter-productive?

Perhaps I need the challenge of selling myself!

FRIDAY, AUGUST 30, 1991

A day of tension again – strong feelings to give-up. Where will all of this take me.

Perhaps I need to focus on where I am, what I am to do. My job is losing focus.

Jesus, give me the ability to be clear and concise with the Bishop – if I end up getting to speak to him.

Jesus, I see you leading me to move. Little else has changed.

Teach me!

SATURDAY, AUGUST 31, 1991

Eating these French Toast Dips and then reading to discover that they have 26 g of fat brings me to realize that in the most innocent ways, we don't even think about caring for ourselves – myself! My body is sacred, but I abuse it. I fight and worry and am tense and fight and worry and am filled with feelings of ill-will. I abuse myself by staying in this situation. How much more do I take? At what point do I call for the cards? An intervention is needed.

I cannot help this being a very consuming situation – one that is almost overwhelming. Is this the context that I withdraw? Should I not rather let – get this issue to be faced.

SUNDAY, SEPTEMBER 1, 1991

To hear about Bill McD not wanting to take sides threw me into a tail spin. No affirmations! No support! Why am I placing so much weight on this. Am I looking for others to be for me – and they can't. After all, if I were strongly for myself, I would truly care for me and move on.

Stronger than ever is the thought pattern that I am powerless, this situation cannot be controlled by me. God, you are in charge of my life! I place myself in your hands.

Yet, I understand and welcome Char's insight that your will for me comes through me. I possess it! I can see if I but look, what is the direction I should take. Jesus, enable me to know myself better. Lift the tensions and the barriers.

Cor ad Cor loquitor!

TUESDAY, SEPEMBER 3, 1991

A better day! More open – activity – distraction! I look ahead to today with a more wholesome mind set.

*But I come to have a queasiness in my gut.
Butterflies! There is so much to be done.*

*I want to be free to look beyond the moment. I
must pave some paths.*

I enter into mystery! That makes me nervous.

Char made a quick, heart-wrenching
response to the all-around negativity toward us at
the Council meeting. She resigned her position as
C.C.D. Director. This meeting stood as a direct
opposite to the gathering on that Spring morning in
1982. The tenor of the parish lay-leaders had taken
a terrible step backwards. Perhaps Char and I had
moved forward too far and too fast!

I destroyed my notes of that evening. The
only audio recording was held by the Council
Chairperson, whose young daughter played it for
our daughter Lynn to explain how bad Char and I
were.

WEDNESDAY, SEPTEMBER 4,1991

*I just read the writing of August 24th. The same
ideas are present, but the fright isn't there. I'm getting
calmer with the thought of moving – leaving Yuma –
settling elsewhere and looking at new possibilities.
Perhaps the thought of growth is becoming stronger.*

*After talking with Dick Felt, I can see myself in
other Church situations. I also can prompt myself to even
look outside of the Church context.*

I can feel a certain freedom rising within me.

Today, I look to the family financial picture that is somewhat bad. What solutions lie here remain to be seen.

TUESDAY, SEPTEMBER 10, 1991

What I embrace, I can let go of too!

To Change the things I can, for, on, in no one, nothing else but myself. Alters adapt, renew, dig out, dig in, anything that makes a difference for me. Stay away from others and theirs!

And the Wisdom, the insight, openness to God, prayerfulness, the ability to listen to my heart and my needs.

To Know the difference. Experience, age, taking time, realize the values involved. Know myself and grow. See the importance in me. Avoid control.

A relief came to me in the presence of Char's change from surgery. Postpone, but perhaps to a better, more settled time for her and us.

The weight of our financial conditions is beginning to weigh down. Time for one pay is nearing.

The wisdom to be prudent and good to self and family.

Jesus, This I need.

WEDNESDAY, SEPTEMBER 11, 1991

Only change I need to be concerned about is myself – I need to examine in an on-going manner, myself!

I have convictions, I need to stand by them.

What are my boundaries?!

THURSDAY, SEPTEMBER 12, 1991

A slow start. Calm

Look to today as a study day!

Set some thoughts down.

Some Liturgy planning ideas!

Here I am – my only point of reference is work! That says much. Prayer – where does it fit in? That's what's prayer's value place – "fit in".

I need to take prayer/focus time today as well. At least, in value, comparable to the above items.

MONDAY SEPTEMBER 16, 1991

I feel dry this morning. The pain of decision rests in me. The support I need is to be found. Where? I look for it from others and I question if it will come. Should I really be looking for/from others?

I'm attempting to take time I want so for you to speak to me lord. I want so to hear! I want You to shout – put a neon sign in front of me. What to do?

I feel very alone – insecure. I don't like it. But it is here!

Jesus, direct my actions today in the will of your way! Truth, Life.

TUESDAY, SEPTEMBER 17, 1991

The pain of indecision! Why again? It won't go away until I grieve! So, says Dick C. do I look to or for more than I need? There is the letting go, the acceptance of a reality that is to be or is not!

I look and seek a note of settlement! Your will is within me! That I may see.

A line for the day, "if you know you're unqualified, you realize you can only accomplish something because you're re-empowered by God."

WEDNESDAY, SEPTEMBER 18, 1991

David's birthday! The mark point of our time at St. Francis – 9 years. Speaking at all the Masses with a freshness, vigor and strength of new beginnings, new life.

Now, as years have passed, the newborn is now growing as child within his own flavor, depth, convictions, sense of survival, and personality. I sit with a sense of wonder at him as well as at myself. What lies ahead? I look to again, a new place and a new start and a new life. Is this real? A vitality, aliveness and strength are present in me that has not been here before.

Anxious, nervous, unsure! Jesus, that I may listen! You are speaking – a break in the wall! That I may be gentle in this journey.

MONDAY, SEPTEMBER 23, 1991

The day begins in the newness. Will it continue with news from Santa Fe? What will that be? How will I respond?

Money issues are on my mind! There are so many areas that need decisions! All I need to do is take one at a time.

Considerations:

Char's surgery

Bankruptcy

Job

- *Looking*
- *Staying*

Santa Fe (if it comes up)

Moving

- *How*
- *When*

Money for all of this

One step/day at a time. Allow all to unfold.

TUESDAY, SEPTEMBER 24, 1991

Char is overcome again by her body. The time for surgery is to be now. No other way!

The emotions of all still run high. Tony's letter is a gem – truthful, yet pointedly strong in the telling sickness, that is present.

I have the fear of so much blowing up in my face! I don't know what, but, I fear, worry! I know that this isn't right – there is my sickness surfacing. Even with the best scene coming. A lot of pain lies ahead.

WEDNESDAY, SEPTEMBER 25, 1991

Life's pain becomes corporal and personal. My back is inflamed. I'm mystified about what started it. Probably a combination of lifting, stress, tension and anything else that comes along.

Deep down I don't like the questioning of whether I should go away. Is this the beginning a realization that you have a call for me here still. That reconciliation is necessary no matter the length of time. Also, needs the realization that financially, survival is more in reach here.

Yet, the greater call may be in the direction of newness, beyond this greater separation from the material things.

THURSDAY, SEPTEMBER 26, 1991

Not being sure is a hard way of life. I sense in Richard, that he is not sure what to do with me. What to talk with me about, ask for input; get things done. He has/is doing what he said others would do – avoid me and lame-duck me.

This back thing is driving me crazy! My control of it is not there. Strong situation to let go.

No doubt the tension/stress of waiting to hear from Santa Fe is also hard to cope with and increases the back frustrations.

As each day has been, what will be new today!?

FRIDAY, SEPTEMBER 27, 1991

*Back doing better – full of medication for pain –
good?*

*Worried that I will have to stay in place and make
a go of it for the new year! What will that mean for Char
and her faith? That's for her – not me.*

Reconciliation?

My job description? My role?

As always, may your will be done!

*The surgery that I journal about is Char's need
for hysterectomy. This personal problem had been
brewing for several months. At this break from work, she
chooses to move ahead with the procedure and its
aftermath of recuperation.*

MONDAY, OCTOBER 7, 1991

*Sincerity, honesty, a sense of purpose is what I
seek. How awesome!*

To continue to identify myself.

*Where is the bottom lie? I see Sharon and a tone
of angers and resentments come to the surface. I blame –
I want to shame her.*

When will it end – to go away?

TUESDAY, OCTOBER 8, 1991

Well, it happened! I have surfaced to the top of the application pile. I am good at what I do and rejoice, and I thank you God for making me who I am. The weakness is here, but also some/many note-worthy strengths.

Yet, in all the joy, I have the tinge of worry, not sure and the somewhat dread level for all the challenges of moving.

The costs and the low salary highlight this area a great deal. The scope of all expands in my mind so much – children, school, friendships, activities.

Yet again, all is not all at once. Pieces are the parts I use, one moment at a time. I cannot take on and hold on to all the children's burdens. I accept them in their pain, encourage them.

As Char said last night, I am loved, touched and graced by the Lord. I walk tall and proud. I make a difference.

Today, I will take care and love myself.

THURSDAY, OCTOBER 10, 1991

To stand on my own! To walk my own path! To speak my words and not just blend with other's.

Venturing forth is in large measure a movement into the involvement with mystery. All that we are going is downward mobility. Some hold this is crazy! Some would view that as running away – Richard –

FRIDAY, OCTOBER 11, 1991

Ups and downs -- in my codependences, Char has set me into a tail-spin again with her downer of a day and evening.

Yet, when I think about it, as soon as chords are touched, I'm set off too. As today's meditation goes, I am all too much living in the past. That I may be present!

Living today means:

Accepting the fact that life is to be difficult for a while.

I can't change Sharon, Richard, Frank, Sr. PR or anyone else involved in the past 2 months.

I can define my thoughts and feelings

I can think and feel positively about moving, hardships, travels, new job, change.

MONDAY, OCTOBER 14, 1991

I so would like to write something provocative, insightful and revealing about the whole situation of the past two months. I want to write it for/to the Council. I want to make clear, get back at, and defend my position. I want to walk away – moving tall yet be in the in-charge – control position.

As I write this, I know in my heart, that it is not the way to go. In some fashion, at a more definite point, I will – need to – share. That a move from here has become valuable in our/my life.

Not is pre-mature. My life situation needs to stabilize – I need to think it all through more. I need to focus on this week – me.

TUESDAY, OCTOBER 15, 1991

In writing the letter yesterday, I felt the anger well within me. The system is faulted – Sr. M.A. is taking the brunt of it – she comes because of it.

My value is to have done the letter, sent it and let it be, even with objection for Char. Not the nice guy! The prospects of it becoming so are slim from perspective.

Lord, your will be done!

WEDNESDAY, OCTOBER 16, 1991

I enter a new world today. Will I stay in it? The next few days will tell. This whole effort is so filled with problems to be solved and issues to be entered. The mysteries really lay here.

Gus' thoughts help! Truly an entering into the passion experience of Jesus! Yet, as Jesus there is light at the end of the tunnel – either a new day elsewhere – Albuquerque or Santa Fe or to take on a new/renewed view of ministry here.

Lord, my Jesus and Christ, grant me the Spirit of Adventure. To leave the comfortable for the not so comfortable – the unknown and different -- to re-cross that desert – to journey to the high-ground.

MONDAY, OCTOBER 21, 1991

What a day yesterday! The confusion negative thinking, and worry held my life in ransom all morning. Breaking the barriers was saying it all to Char – she is being accepting in a complete understanding way meant so much! Relief. By days end a whole fresh outlook of freedom came over me.

One major insight – the enmeshment of my work and life has been destructive to say the least. The conviction to write of my thoughts and feelings is a rewarding feeling.

Last night the Gospel said to me – follow by my path! One that will not contain power, possessions and prestige!

"It is more difficult to be free than not be free." It isn't running away, its embracing.

TUESDAY, OCTOBER 22, 1991

Wait! What for? An expression of God's will!? Will it come today? If not, what will/should I do?

I do resolve to begin preparing a statement – this is necessary if I go or stay! It will be difficult, not my "first draft, only draft" approach. At least I don't think so.

Lord, bless this day. Allow me to recognize your presence, hand, and will running through it. Grant me peace.

Money matters too! What a step – bankrupt! . .

In the meantime, I applied for a position in the religious education department of the Archdiocese of Santa Fe, New Mexico. I went there for an interview that was a valuable uplift to my self-appreciation. The Director seemed to be very pleased by my know-how in dealing with various problematic areas, of ministry, and of the formation of catechetical leaders. There was, however, another local candidate up for the position who was better known to parish ministers. The ransom wait continued at least a little longer.

Chapter Six

An End and a New Beginning

Although our hopes were for a move to Santa Fe, I could not overcome the local candidate who was better known to the church leadership and in the end, she was selected for the position. The hiring committee's area of concern with me was that my theological training was too old. Such is life.

I outline some of the feelings I had learning this news in these next journal entries, and in the days ahead, our struggle continued as I sought a solution to our future.

TUESDAY, OCTOBER 29, 1991

The waiting ended. The results are not favorable. A no! a first! What lies ahead? How to regain, acquire, maintain a serenity – a clear acceptance coupled with courage.

In all this journey remains a pain – it appears that a wholeness, a completeness will not arrive at all, or, least, in short order. Char is not going to change her outlook toward Church/attending very soon. Sharon isn't going to depart quickly or without a push. The dysfunctions of the whole situation will not be changed.

WEDNESDAY, OCTOBER 30, 1991

A no is hard to take. The outside approval isn't there. I need to look within myself! What are my qualities? My gifts? I must go back and examine myself – goals, directions? What is the value of me?

All this is important, but what is essential is that I accept the fact that the greatness of me is within me. I don't have to depend on others for my worth.

The remainder of 1991 moves along in a steadily evolving process of good days, not so good times, and strong challenged periods of living.

WEDNESDAY, NOVEMBER 27, 1991

Love of self. When I am full of anger, pain, emptiness, aloneness, imprisonment, I am not taking care of myself. I am holding on, savoring, revenging and dying for control. This realization, new thought hit last night. In all that I am preparing to do, I am getting back. I will lose control of the situation. Making or taking a stand, what does this mean? I need to opt into this. What is it that will break my brokenness and usher in wholeness.

To have all neatly packaged is probably beyond possibilities. What is left?

SATURDAY, NOVEMBER 30, 1991

Gentle acceptance of self! A feeling of wholeness is coming to me.

A sense of letting go and forgiving is a stronger reality. Deep down there is a lingering insecurity = unsureness, but that's OK too.

I look to today as a time for a few things to do – to be.

A consideration that weight is eating – habits that I'm getting back to – weight gain – poor health – higher cholesterol! What to do? The discipline needed! The sense of self-respect, love, recognizing that which is outside of my control. Here again, what to do?

Perhaps I'm into too much alone time – I become vulnerable to myself and my inclinations. My body – I – need to be cleansed. To become whole again – to recognize and accept myself.

MONDAY, DECEMBER 2, 1991

Advent – sure will be different this year – cutting back – slowing down – leaving the race of our time – attempting to be in the pattern of the Body of Christ – being ready for the call – the coming to be. To reflect on the holy ground, the sacred place of His being – in with, and through me.

Letting go and letting God lead and draw and bring me is of essential importance. Let the grieving process go on.

Today, attend to the Lord, his people, myself, Char, the family.

Jesus, let peace of confidence and faith reign in my heart. Let the clutter not mix and nullify the beauty of the moments.

WEDNESDAY, DECEMBER 4, 1991

"I will never deny you!" I just read these words and they are yours Jesus to me. A consolation – a hope – a source of strength.

Jesus, you care about me and you love me most directly, be with me in this day of work, listening, giving.

I am touched by the need, value, spiritual discipline to care for myself in eating and exercising. I make and have made many resolutions in this direction. Jesus, I give my power to be with your power for me in this regard.

TUESDAY, DECEMBER 24, 1991

Up early! Can't sleep! Too much food. A lesson? I'm the only one who can take care of myself.

A busy day – too soon! Very long. Why – even in our slow down mode? Last minutes! If money not in, then this wouldn't be. Teach me, Lord. Really, I know that but I need to listen. Today, I can say mania! Tomorrow to sit and wait.

- *Shopping*
- *Wrapping*
- *Baking*
- *Cleaning*
- *Bathroom*
- *Window*
- *Sitting out in Church*

- *Shower and shave and dress*

THURSDAY, DECEMBER 26, 1991

I just read this day a year ago. How much is the same, yet, there ARE significant differences – tired, anger, pushing, closeness, tiredness, hopes. This AM has brought all into healing as Brian and I laughed, joked and surrendered to the situation that we couldn't change. We survived. We grew, I'm sure. The Son shines on us.

I'll work a little today and I'll be for others as best as I can!

Thank you, Jesus! A hope of a new day!

SATURDAY, DECEMBER 29, 1991

I'm struck this AM with the question mark: Where? When? Why? How do I leave this in God's hands? Where do I settle myself? How strong do I make my commitments? All these? Makes me uncomfortable!

Welcoming guests. A new, or renewed horizon!

Be at Peace!!

Wherever, However, whenever you lead me I will go! A profession of faith that remains strong!

I begin 1992 with an innocence of heart, a vision of ministry that needs development, and a hope of a new dawning day, year! The Grand Canyon still needs to be met, admired and bravely crossed through.

MONDAY, JANUARY 6, 1992

The insight of my time with Dick has been the idea that the person I am having difficulty with is mirroring me for me. I look at Richard as being very concerned about being in charge, being the identified one, the one in role of responsibility looked to all as pastor-boss. I like all of that. I want that level of working. I picture myself in this role. I want – desire the priesthood. I could do it better, certainly as well as. I challenge him. I continue to want to! I want to let him feel that he isn't doing all as he should!

Control is the name of the game. Mine, his, who's? All that I see in him, I see in myself.

This time of life thing is significant. We all look for the same. Can we admit this and blend and prosper?

TUESDAY, JANUARY 7, 1992

Another day! Each day displays your love, care, challenge and costly grace. Kathy's death! What a shock!

The weaving thought – why her at such a young age – alone?

Char writes beautifully of her legacy – that which she leaves behind. A gift freely given, she hands on.

To hold on to Kathy's spirit, peace, sense of ease, ability to grab beauty and share it.

Another patron of our programs! Saints of our day – Barbara, Jennifer, Katherine!

We praise God as he has given us them, to walk the same path we have walked.

The new year brought a freeing day near mid-January where I experienced an important moment of confidence where I profoundly remembered death, tension, sadness, hope, nerves, successes, and worries all has been of Jesus. And through it all, Jesus, you have walked alongside me. Char's abandoned church work combined with my own has given us great freedom to enjoy. We experienced a sense of well-being only overshadowed by our pressing need for financial security and a sense of finding our place. Staying put did not feel like a real possibility yet it was tempting as I sought discernment and wisdom in deciding our next steps.

THURSDAY, JANUARY 16, 1992

Char is off and running! Would that all were different. May You watch over us and especially Char, as we attempt to live our lives. May we be whole! Show us the way! Place the paving stones in our path.

Frustration of the day will arise. May I turn to You – You are my peace and hope.

Rain down a gentle sense of hope on Char. Let her lungs hold.

FRIDAY, JANUARY 17, 1992

Char had such a hard night. The sureness about moving is strong. I have spent myself here. The closeness to Church here, not only in physical distance, but also in moral closeness, has harmed our outlook. If Char hadn't quit, we would have gone mad. Literally.

No matter how long it takes, it is time to go! I can't control! That's a beauty. Let Go! God, you lead. Inspire my day!

The early weeks and months of this year escorts a wide variety of questions, possibilities and demands upon me. Char and I have spoken often and concluded that all steps need to be taken by me to discover another ministry situation to fulfill the call to serve the Church community that the Lord has made for us.

These next journal entries reflect the heartache, the discernment, and the real difficult effort to leave behind St. Francis and Yuma.

THURSDAY, JANUARY 30, 1992

The realization of moving on after 10 years is strengthening!

I need to appreciate myself a great deal more. My giftedness – organizing! I should not negate myself as I do.   Even though it is in my mind – I still do!

MONDAY, FEBRUARY 3, 1992

A weekend again. Slow – good! Char remains poor – breathing, etc. Dr. Today!

As I look to the week ahead, I find a feeling of hopefulness – meet John and Joe in Phoenix. Possibilities? Self-selling! I can do it!

Jesus, I look to today with the hope of rest, enjoying the time I have and yet, being fresh to reach out to the folks and youth that I meet with tonight.

As I watch the couple next to me, I pray that Char and I may grow older gracefully!

THURSDAY, FEBRUARY 13, 1992

Change – to do it often is to grow. After 10 years – the need is clear to go on! There is fear, hope, anger, joy, adventure, pain, insecurity and purpose about it all. It's a step off the edge that many won't understand or accept.

Relating to my brothers over the issue of money and living-style, remains a real challenge and opportunity.

Getting there – a job – will be most of the trial. At some point, need to move more strongly!

MONDAY, MARCH 2, 1992

Ready! Lent – 2 days away! My sincere prayer is to take hold of Char's thoughts about consecrating the moment, letting the now be binding enough. To live in, into and through each day in the presence of the LORD. Not needed to take on more, but to be!

MONDAY, MARCH 16, 1992

A Dream! I'm in a condo setting. Len lives there. In going to his place, I begin to recognize Jim Landy, as a married man. He is golfing – teeing off from a patio out over a hilly valley. Len is sitting talking with him – I stop to speak with and greet. He embraces me.

What does this mean? I felt when I awoke – a freedom, freshness, a hope that the past is moving aside, and new beginnings are to happen. No longer confined to the past of the seminary – the old way. The prospects of new work lie ahead.

THURSDAY, MARCH 26, 1992

Power comes in many forms. For me yesterday it was as feelings of sadness, powerlessness, mixed with worry and concern that the solution to issues is not an easy journey. There will be great – on-going amounts of letting go.

The waiting to hear from Henderson, the lack – in fact, the low – of money flow, Char's condition, her poor work situation, all these, are a burden to me – MY LENT.

To know that you love me unconditionally is a boast. Jesus, grace me to go beyond the knowledge to the feeling of this love.

TUESDAY, MARCH 31, 1992

Yesterday – to be joyful – to be affirmed – to be excited – to be energized – to be confident -- to be worthy! The "I am..." test was self-lifting. I am! I don't have to just do.

I look ahead – even, dangerously living into the future. I must be very careful – that can ruin me – the present is my on-going challenge. My best prep for wherever is now!

Jesus, thank you for this experience of rejuvenation!

JUNE 1! Summer begins, but spring hasn't yet cleared out the winter. The invitation arrived for both Char and me to interview at Corpus Christi parish and school in Colorado Springs. It was a proclamation that the Lord reigned in our lives.

THURSDAY, JUNE 4, 1992

Well. What a week. Back on the plane – to home – Yuma. To say good-bye! The surprises of the Lord have not stopped! From interview early, the ease, the welcome, the acceptance, the teaching position in choice grade, the money. Will it stop. How exciting!

One day at a time. Putting closure on things will not be easy. Grief. Harsh, but real.

I believe it will be important for me to journal daily now to work at staying in touch with myself and what I'm doing or how I'm feeling.

FRIDAY, JUNE 5, 1992

I'm back in Carl's Jr. Home becomes a passing scene now. A journey marker. Going-on.

In the Lord's hands:

> *Char's fees for two good courses*
>
> *Bills to handle*
>
> *Moving*
>
> **House Sale*

We place Bri, Lynn, and Dave in your hands as we journey through all these movements that are hard. Give char and I the courage to be askers – Doug

Frank, and anyone else we can think of

I thank you Jesus, for unfolding this path for us.

We place this before you, Lord! Take care of it. Help me to let go of it. You have brought us this far, You will not let us go. The signs are too strong.

In the path of seeking financial support, I approach Fr. Frank. He will help me but asks me to take on a project that will assist St. Francis to continue the work of Evangelization. My composition, paper, program, was very detailed and complete. I left no stone unturned as the month of June and early July races by.

Today, in retrospect, I remember feeling successful in Yuma. Of course, I made some enemies and frankly, did some stupid things myself. But, I had a lot of good friends and people who thought the same way as I did, and that helped a lot. But most of all, it was Char; Char was more of a support system than I even thought possible going through life.

WEDNESDAY, JULY 15, 1992

The pages have turned! How much has happened, been unraveled, been revealed. The Lord cares for us and will continue to do so! He holds us!

Since last writing some great things have happened – Frank project completed, money came in from him, Doug and Russ. He who seeks, finds.

Work over – parties held – farewells said, packing in process -Char's course over and very successfully enriching!

The House remains in your hands. Your plan will prevail for us. In your time – Give me, Jesus the gift of waiting in Faith.

Thank you, Jesus! You hold us in the Palm of Your Hand!

We count down the days! The U-Haul and the car are ready to go. The whole situation is summed up as two young men embrace in the street, crying on each other's shoulder and step apart. The shield is broken open. David and Adam say their goodbyes! Remember! They have just completed the third Grade and have been close since pre-school.

We are on our way!

The story of our journey took us through some back roads to the Grand Canyon. This was our first visit there after ten years in Arizona. We were awestruck. What a sight! Our time there was brief, but we all concluded that we will be back!

Chapter Seven

New Beginnings

I am very hard on myself. It's the nature of the beast. Am I still that way? Probably to some degree. Sadly, I made a mess of our family finances over the course of the whole span of our lives and we were forced into bankruptcy in January of 1992. With the big crinkle of needing to move out of Yuma after the whole parish situation blew up in our face the year before, life was stressful. And then, there was Charlotte's hysterectomy right after that.

I began to believe six to seven years is good to be at any Church home. Any more than that? Things can happen that are not always very good. That's what happened in Yuma. We were there 10 years. The pastor had been there 8 years longer for a total of 18 years. After we left, he stayed a year or two longer before he also left. First, he took a sabbatical and then went off to school. When he returned, he found a home in a Tucson parish. These next journal entries highlight the arrival in Colorado Springs, CO and our subsequent assignment in the Phoenix area.

MONDAY, AUGUST 10, 1992

Many days – many miles! We are here – in the place where we are. To be holy, to be in Your will. Sacred is this ground.

Yet, life is filled with tensions, newness, strangeness and all the other aspects of change.

Jesus, this day begins work! A slow start – yet it is to be day 1! My approach: Settle in! Write some priorities, even as I unpack.

In the matters of home – may my contacts be of benefit. We believe that a house we like, will be placed in our hands for our grace in this place. A step-in faith, a leap of Hope!

Embrace Char this day with renewal of heart! Let the water flow!'

Give Brian a keen eye, a calm grip and a secure confidence in this very new environment.

David, Jesus, touch deeply to be healed, to thrive in his sensitive nature, and to trust that he is special.

Lynn, our young-lady. May she discover friendship anew!

A Misstep!

Something very telling is happening now. I do not have any journal entry for this time UNTIL LATE December. Why? In this period, I found myself entrapped in my own web of misjudgments, poor moves, and false-pride. Street crossing was not a "walk in the park"! There were barriers for me to face and persons to battle in this new adventure. I was stopped in mid-street!

My ministry at Corpus Christi Church in Colorado Springs, Colorado began with a very good retreat/planning week in the beautiful mountains outside the city. My family settled into a lesser quality motel to wait for me. Char had her parenting skills questioned by several motel staff persons who were very inconsiderate, rude, and judgmental.

She moved to another place that proved to be bearable for another two nights. Her days were spent finding an apartment for us to call home.

My experience with the Church staff was positive and promising. The Youth Minister and myself were new while the Liturgy Director, Social Issues Coordinator, Parish Administrator and School Principal were "old-timers" working with the Pastor. They seemed to be on a secure, equal footing.

I entered in with a batch of ideas gleaned from my years in Yuma. In theory, I believed that I entered the history book of this parish and I needed to discover what page I was on and absorb the setting for my ministry. As the weeks went by, I forgot all that and pursued "my better idea". With the Youth Minister at my side, I marched ahead proposing, pushing and pulling the staff to accept my plans for adopting a new approach for OCIA, incorporating Liturgy of the Word for Children at a Sunday Mass, and more family involvement in the preparation and celebration of the Sacraments, Eucharist and Reconciliation. At the same time, Susan made several up-dating approaches to youth ministry. Nothing was ever strongly disputed at staff meetings. All appeared to be moving on a progressive trend.

Then, in early Advent, the pastor asked Susan and me to sit down with him. He shared his displeasure with us and the need for us to slow down with "new" ways. He felt that we were pushing him away from involvement in the projects that were going on in our respective ministries. No one else on the staff acted in such a fashion. I decided to hold back some plans I was making to refresh the catechesis of children and junior-high youth.

I learned that I did not have the pastor's ear as I had in Yuma.

I was used to having Richard stop in at my office to chat, and agree or disagree, on plans and issues of concern.

Here, Gerry, unknown to me, expected that I should come to him and get his O.K. even before any discussion at a staff meeting. This meeting was to be over his breakfast table after 8 AM Mass. I didn't go for this approach! With all else that was altered in our family's life, there were too many demands that were very different than life in Yuma.

WEDNESDAY, DECEMBER 30, 1992

First Thoughts of the day! Why is this happening to us? Such strong feelings of unrest. Jesus, brother and Lord, are you trying to tell us something? Where and What do you want of us? Little seems to be working for us! Money is this the answer. NO, but it would relieve the pressure. Work enters it all, also.

THURSDAY, DECEMBER 31, 1992

Yesterday was such a downer! House sale hopes are dim. Why? Are we being called to let go of it all? On this last day – not interested in looking back, I still hope for new days. The work – Church situation still hangs as well. What will the new year bring there? All so – so negative! May the sun burn away the veil of fog to open the hillside!

Richard Bergkessel

FRIDAY, JANUARY 1, 1993

Well, we start over! What's this mean each 365 days. Surely it hasn't been an uplifting end of the year past. Now to look ahead. The sun is shining! May the hope we rely on continue to shine for us.

May Char and I discover encouragement for one another. We need a breakthrough – Let us Lord, be sharp to see it happening.

SATURDAY, JANUARY 2, 1993

It appears as a pit, a hole, that will consume us. Being poor is a road that will not stop. It's "middle-class" poverty. Put up a show. Do things as usual. Don't let on. All is O.K. The lie is living. It's so hard to face! To have hope! Bless us Jesus! Gift us with a trusting, confident, firm, hope in Your care! May we understand your revelation.

SUNDAY, JANURY 3, 1993

Epiphany! Showing and Telling! Getting back to it! For RICA, only 2 show up for the session – discouraging! What lies ahead? New ideas need to unfold. The Lord's Day and Year! Turning all over to Him is the key! Jesus, let me see! Footprints in the Sand.

MONDAY, JANUARY 4, 1993

School starts! Getting at an almost totally work focus again. Even at best – all equal – we will just about break even on our wages. Can this long endure? I'm tiring of the on-going material concerns that occupy my attention. Jesus, help me to get on with my life! May you

*touch others that all pans out in Yuma! Jesus be my
strength!*

TUESDAY, JANUARY 5, 1993

*At prayer, Christine! It prompts some hope that
the object of ministry is service – youth/families/people!
New direction and new outlooks are a key. My strong
feelings of separateness from Gerry need a healing nod!
How? Talk is important. This coupled with home and
money issues is really rocking us! Jesus, hold us! Let your
touch be felt.*

WEDNESDAY, JANURY 6, 1993

*The mood! Upbeat and depressing. Both are in
me! An Epiphany Day. Uncle Frank/Death. Fr. B and
staff issues/Commission of Hope and Excitement. A
rut/new ideas. Will it all come together? I don't know. But
that is O.K. Let's talk about it. Will that come? I need to
be resourced! Where will it come from? I don't like being
in just a compartment.*

THURSDAY, JANUARY 7, 1993

*Another day of adventure! Gerry and Dom – what
will be? Carry out some clearing of air. The beginning of
Reconciliation! To look at the health of conflict. PM. Not
real positive – CONTROL is the name of the game. Do I
hold out or fold? How? Jesus, that your light shine on me.*

FRIDAY, JANUARY 8, 1993

(Full Moon) this explains parts! Snowing in a fair fashion. Good news on the house process in Yuma. May it proceed in a timely fashion. Details of our movement here will abound. I'm inclined to see how the next month comes and goes. Is this real?

Talking over the plan is to be on-going. Can I do it? Do I want to do it? Why do it? Kissing up? Enlightenment! Face the season!

SATURDAY, JANUARY 9, 1993

How awful I feel – I don't like conflict! I don't' like feeling used, I feel very constricted – held in check! As I've been writing all week – what's the way out? I can't focus on work – skipping todays' workshop – yet, I can't stop thinking about it all.

SUNDAY, JANUARY 10, 1993

I am writing this on Monday morning. It looks like I need to do it early or it won't be done. A real hanging over AM until I was done. I was the actor on a stage. When I was done, there was a relief. I can't believe the overriding passive. It's been always present through the weekend. I feel, at the moment, that there is no way out, but out! Am I lacking something? So many thoughts run through my head. I've made the wrong move! This is really hard to say and to accept. How much more sensitive I need to become. How do I do that? I want to compromise, see all benefit of view and keep everyone happy. Jesus, bless me in my day's discussion etc.

TUESDAY, JANUARY 12, 1993

The saga continues! I'll see Kathy H at the diocese today! Where will all this take me – lead me? Jesus, you know, I don't. I continue to let go – you are in charge. My power is less. I work at doing my best! I feel very alone this AM, Jesus, I hope, I trust you will walk with me. I am afraid. What will happen to us? Jesus, may I feel your touch.

WEDNESDAY, JANUARY 13, 1993

I saw Kathy! Just talking has helped. Meeting was typical! Unclear, unsure, evasive! Power rests on Pastor! Easy! We lose all sense of the communal. Hope continues to spring as Kathy knows I'm looking around.

THURSDAY, JANUARY 14, 1993

The day dawns more forcefully! A Freshness stands as I decide that I will be myself! I will do my thing, report my doings and promote them. I will look and consider change. The hope I have rests in me! Jesus, you have set it there if I but look, I will see and be. Anoint my searching and seeking.

SUNDAY, JANUARY 17, 1993

Again, I move through these days! Sat. was a roller-coaster. The end was a pit. (Base with 1 sq. with pockets empty.) Another 3 months to wait. Money coming soon, but that covers 3,000 and nothing more. I've become so edgy and depressed. How to stem this, I'm unsure at the moment. I look to outside facts, happenings and things but deep down, I know it's not there.

MONDAY, JANUARY 18, 1993

Martin Luther King, Jr. Day

Today, we celebrate a martyr who had to have such times in his life.

As yesterday moved along, I recognized that I need to risk, expand my work view and seek out new possibilities. Church has limited me and I'm not sure this is where I should stay. Jesus be my guide – discover with me our Father's will.

TUESDAY, JANUARY 19, 1993

Blah mood! Bless David. Be with Brian. Encourage Lynn. The start of 2nd half! Easy come/Easy go spirit. What will spark me? The word of the weekend – insecurity! A long road is ahead of us in any regard. Where does my faith spring? The weaving thought – now is the time to move away from Church focus entirely.

WEDNESDAY, JANUARY 20, 1993

What a day yesterday was! Long, drawn, really high-lighting the change mode that is needed. To depart from church isn't really what I want – but to be in a situation that is welcoming, calling forth skills, and collaboratively focused. Good to hear from Sherlyn, and Yuma. Money pressures hang on! Jesus, inspire my gift of hope.

THURSDAY, JANUARY 21, 1993

Fast pace start to the day! Dentist!! A real sense of hope in approaching a change. What are my possibilities? Jesus, - I give myself and all of this over to you. Make of it what you will – allow me to see the peace! Lead me on!

FRIDAY, JANUARY 22, 1993

Constantly look to well-founded Hope! He holds us in the palm of his hand! Very humbling – asked for money for shopping and prescriptions. How long can we go along at this level? Change and betterment is essential. The feeling is strong that we are socked in and the limits are here.

As I reflect on these days, they were times of many blessings and the power of God's grace. Char, Brian, Lynn, David and I found a real bond in the tight budget of Christmas, the generous gifting by the school faculty and the closeness that occurred in our little family circle. We rejoiced in a Christmas Eve dinner at a steak house; opening gifts on Christmas Eve for the first time, and having a party-like event after evening Mass.

Even in these early days of 1993, after only five months at Corpus Christi, I began to see the hand-writing on the wall. This place for ministry was not going to work for me, and in turn, for the parish. Before Lent started that year, Fr. Gerry asked me through the parish administrator to discontinue the Liturgy of the Word for children. There were safety issues with the children in the Church basement.

We gave our younger son, David, the choice to remain in the city school or come to his mother's small class at Corpus Christi School. He chose his Mom's class. Char was really thrilled, and David became his non-worrisome self again. Brian enjoyed golf all year around. He improved and impressed many adult men with his talent. Lynn embraced her school and class, making several good girl-friends.

Char and I talked for hours about our future here, elsewhere, and how we could afford any situation. I started to find other local parish opportunities, with little luck. Char started to seek-out public-school positions for the coming year. All-in-all, we were living a stressful style of life. As an outlet, we found a budget movie theater, where, as a family, we went about twice a month.

Mixed with work issues, the house we were renting became a cause for panic. The owners began to pressure us to buy it. They began to demand that we move out or buy. Somehow, they found out that our money from the Yuma house came through and we had $3,000 in our bank account.

All things in Colorado Springs came to a halt on the Ides of March, the 15th, when the parish administrator stopped into my office to tell me that I was not welcomed back for next year. There were irreconcilable differences between the pastor and me.

The next morning very early, I woke up, went down to watch the sun rising and wrote the following poem.

The Resurrection Moment

I believe there's a Resurrection
Moment coming.
Until then the passion – days
Continue.
The Falls are very real and surely
Will be more than three for me.
The ropes are strong. The nails are
Sharp. The whip stings.
A Resurrection moment
is coming.
The crowd grows louder and the
Tearing comments become more
Intense.
It's all up – hill!
Is this your will?
It is your way! It's redemption,
A saving event.
A Resurrection moment
Is coming.
Jesus, allow the tears, sweat,
And blood of feeling, emotion
And thought leave me.
Even as with you!
I believe there's a Resurrection
Moment coming!

The next two months were very difficult to handle. The owners of our home wanted to put it on the market; Char and I couldn't button up a job; David, Lynn and Brian felt very insecure as we stumbled along.

I chose a brief segment of my journal to express the turmoil and possible outcome.

TUESDAY, MAY 11, 1993

Another day! Highs and Lows! Turning to Yuma! House issue. How will it all work out? Help! Is there anyone – here for us? Really? I don't think so!

Jesus, please make yourself known to us in a clear way, open doors. Where, when, how, who, on and on to go! Jesus, Light a light in me, us!!!

WEDNESDAY, MAY 12, 1993

Such tensions! Chest hurts! The thought of moving borders on overwhelm. The turns have been an on-going limit move! Constriction is the word of the year. What will today bring? Jesus, I beg you to open a door! The thought of moving right now is impossible. But you see the whole picture. Light our way with another piece of the puzzle.

THURSDAY, MAY 13, 1993

The pain of nerves for me – indigestion! How on top of it do I need to get for Tuesday interview. House rental hunting. How unfulfilling it all is. There seems to be so much pressure. When, how will there be relief? Jesus, touch our lives today as we look at this apartment --- as we share with the kids – as we continue to job search! Your will be done, but also be made known to us.

FRIDAY, MAY 14, 1993

So, varied a day! My reading was very powerful for me as well as for many people. Yet as the day ended, the pressures of all became so real. Then, Chandler AZ's call – what a surprise and what a challenge.

Char's point of going into this with two jobs is absolute. If it is Your will, then all will fall into place.

SATURDAY, MAY 15, 1993

Telling Lynn and Dave remain. The whole moving scene is scary and overwhelming. One week and we are out! we have so much to face – Do this with us Jesus. Keep me calm and at peace with your will as it unfolds. I pray Coda will be a blessing.

My responsibilities at Corpus Christi did not go away. I had to plan the celebration of the Easter Vigil with the initiation of several adults into the church. First Communion for the children in third grade needed to be planned and prepared for with parents and children. My heart was not centered in these efforts. Guilt level was high. I could not rise above my human condition! I worked very hard to not mix my feelings of dislike for parish leaders and the ministry of service to this group of persons and families.

The Resurrection moment dawns. In quick succession, I receive a call from St. Andrew the Apostle in Chandler, Arizona. They would like to interview me as soon as possible. The parish needs an adult formation director! Our hopes are raised for yet another change.

Chapter Eight

St. Andrews

Like most American teenagers, the secular rite of passage of learning to drive is exciting and terrifying. It was no different this year when we launched Brian into the eight-week preparation.

David discovered the world of nature's beauty during this same time in an away place where he begins work on a "fort" and Lynn began a valued friendship with a classmate. She also won the classroom prize of the frozen-yogurt treat with her teacher. For each of our children, these important milestones became valued reasons to stay put in Colorado.

Beginning on May 25th, our family then experienced one of the most eventful single months of our lives! Follow along as I attempt to condense this time into a digestible fashion.

TUESDAY, MAY 25, 1993

I travel to Chandler, AZ to be interviewed by St. Andrew's parish staff. This proved to be a wonderful experience and the team there received me with open arms. In fact, relief reigns as I am hired on the spot.

WEDNESDAY, May 26, 1993

The very next day, I am back at home. Char and I discuss my experience and together, we experienced confidence and a eagerness to look ahead.

105

Richard Bergkessel

In the excitement, we did not ask every question and those that we did ask, were not all answered.

SATURDAY, MAY 29, 1993

A few days later, countless details and particulars began to stall and confound us. Three days later, Char and I grow caught up and we then failed to rejoice in the large picture before us. These are dangerous waters.

SUNDAY, MAY 31, 1993

It's Memorial Day and we learn Char's dad is very near death. We decide to travel to Ohio to see him before he dies.

MONDAY, JUNE 1, 1993

Char, Lynn and I leave for Cleveland, one day after learning the news.

TUESDAY-THURSDAY, JUNE 2-4, 1993

We are blessed when we arrive to be able to spend time with Dad/Grandpa.

FRIDAY, JUNE 5, 1993

Char is with her Dad today as he passes.

MONDAY, JUNE 8, 1993

Today is the day of celebration of Resurrection for George Gedeon, Char's father. His life is not ended, but has merely changed.

TUESDAY, JUNE 9, 1993

We return to Colorado Springs.

Upon our return, we learn Brian has a surprise for us. And it was not a good one. While we were gone, he and two friends took our car from the garage and were driving around. The police stopped them while they parked at a convenience store. It seems one of Brian's friends was driving suspiciously, raising the ire of the police. He was underage and did not own a license.

Brian was very frightened about what we would do when we learned this. Sadly, his only idea of how a parent responds to a situation such as this was what happened to his friend who was caught driving without a license--A father repeatedly punched and kicked his son to the ground and to continue to punch and kick him.

Our reaction to learning this terrifying news was to simply hold Brian and let him cry. What's worse is Brian was very sick with a cold and fever. He was completely overwhelmed and incredulous of our understanding approach to this incident and our acceptance of him over several days of discussion.

SATURDAY, JUNE 13, 1993

Moving day. Our move to Arizona is here; we now leave the natural beauty of this area behind, for the uniquely different beauty of the Valley of the Sun.

SUNDAY, JUNE 14, 1993

We arrive in Chandler and our temporary home for two weeks, a Days Inn. It's part of the process and together, we will make the best of it.

MONDAY-WEDNESDAY, June 15 – 17, 1993

We spent every waking moment house shopping for three days. Finally, we signed a contract for a modest home in a development of tract houses--something to call our own. We sought approval from and received it from the children before we signed.

FRIDAY-SUNDAY, JUNE 19 – 24, 1993

The day arrives where we close on our new home. Over the coming days, we move ourselves in and sleep on the floor until our things arrive. Sunday comes and along with it, the movers. Our month-long saga over several states is complete and we go about the business of setting up our new home which will serve as the centerpiece of our lives for the next several years.

In July of 1993, I begin my work at St. Andrew the Apostle. It's the seventh place I've worked during my career in the Church.

It was one of the fastest growing parishes in the Phoenix Diocese and its pastor, Fr. Joe, and Sr. Pat and now, I, were the only long-term, professionally-trained staff. The others were prepared in an on-the-job fashion over the years since the parish begin in 1985.

I was still, very much reeling from the Corpus Christi experience. From that, I felt alone, nervous, very unsure of myself and yet, I felt that I had to appear firm and confident upon my entrance.

These next journal entries over the early weeks of settling in, speak much about my mood and about how our family was settling in.

TUESDAY, JULY 13, 1993

I'm paying the price of being unknown. The feelings of being less-than are a big battle! With NO CAR and I am extremely limited with little recourse, but to beg. Jesus. Show me the way to go. Strengthen my inner power.

WEDNESDAY, JULY 14, 1993

How very hard yesterday was! Car – Rental – Feeling very dumb, stupid and ugly! The whole Corpus Christi thing springs up. Anger, regret again, and feeling put down. I call the church – The Bishop – into question and I quickly get into what I should have done! I want to beat a dead horse. I want to be utterly strong and withstand all of this. Yet another day brings new hopes and struggles! Jesus be with me!

THURSDAY, JULY 15, 1993

The beginning of a day of greater peace. The tension Char has is strong and the hardship she bears here in the desert – the air quality and the danger it seems to her system-is challenging. The practical items take so much effort, of the mind, at least. Looking ahead to tomorrow and going to Yuma. How unusual! We run away and now I'm driving back. The utter mystery of Your Plan!

FRIDAY, JULY 16, 1993

Re-meeting old friends! A treasure in them as they remind me of the treasure in me. I am good, creative and together in so many ways. It takes time – I need to give myself this time all the time. I feel like I'm really enjoying my history. All this applies to the future. May I learn from my past.

SATURDAY, JULY 17, 1993

The realities of a problematic life are here too. As Nancy said, to move is good, to see what we've been is to grow and learn. A little reading in here. A new frontier lies ahead – a sense of hope is engendered within me, what it takes. No need to push and be forceful – it will all evolve.

MONDAY, JULY 19, 1993

A refreshing weekend of affirmation. A ray of hope that I have within me of what it takes to minister, to be successful and to relate to people at their level.

Jesus, I thank you. Continue to be grace in me, with me and from me. May this week unfold in a healthy fashion!

TUESDAY, JULY 20, 1993

A very long day yesterday! Meeting sets a stage for some on-going education and development for RCIA Team. Counter the past. Yet, there is a resource here of experience that enriches me and gives me a sense of belonging. Give us the strength as a family to continue to settle in. Gift Char with health! Guard her in all ways! Especially to land a teaching job.

THURSDAY, JULY 22, 1993

Taking a day off needs control and direction! I can easily not become refreshed! I look at too much, too fast. I need to be looking at myself and you, Jesus! Being busy about so much is not to anyone's benefit. To a certain degree, yesterday became a blur!

FRIDAY, JULY 23, 1993

Char takes the lead – letter Gerry! She puts out so much more than she recognizes. A real form of blessing! This letter continues the pains that are still a part of our system as a family. The persistent WHY is haunting. Jesus, guide our day – open doors and especially give Char an uplift!

SUNDAY, JULY 25,1993

New resolves – exercise, lose weight, eat better! In all, I need to take better care of myself! Yesterday's Stinking thinking really can wear one down. I need to come to loving me enough to take the space necessary to be clear about decisions. Only in the family circle do I judge rather poorly. Jesus, inspire this day to be calm and collected! Be with Char in lifting her up!

MONDAY, JULY 26, 1993

I feel a real freshness! Perhaps walking helps. The on-going task of getting use to all! Remain gunshy. Probably will be for a while!? The reality of our need to streamline spending is settling on me. Jesus, unfold in our lives the glimpse of your mystery working in, around, and through us.

TUESDAY, JULY 27, 1993

The beauty of early morning! Truly to wish that Char had something to focus on – a position, interview, etc. Jesus, bless this pocket for Chandler. Another road! May it be open and workable. Charge her spirit. May I have the focus to go for it as this day evolves. Open Bruggeman's heart sensibilities to our situation. Inspire me today!

THURSDAY, JULY 29, 1993

Back to skipping my day off. Maybe I'll get in gear. My heart goes out to Char as she suffers through the rough moments of breathing. May the climate and weather and life setting be acceptable to her. Thank you,

Jesus in enriching me as I minister in various ways. Even amid the good things, I recognize the need to be held in Your hands!

FRIDAY, JULY 30, 1993

Pay day! It's great to get going with exercise! Praise you God as you give Char a sense of well-being and livelihood. Continue to bless her – especially with a job situation. It surely will help all of us in the life-style line. Thank you, Jesus, for the gift to be still, to relax and to move along with relative peace.

SUNDAY, AUGUST 1, 1993

I am here in Chandler introducing myself! A year ago, we arrived in Colorado Springs to begin anew! A real-life adventure. Amid introductions, I'm remaining stuck on the long challenge – WHY am I here? Why not still in Colorado Springs? I'm saying: "Come follow me" – how strongly do I believe this? Be with us Jesus!

MONDAY, AUGUST 2, 1993

Ah!!!! Hot days and taxing experiences. The long drive to Dateland with David drained all energy. New day possibilities in this month two of work draw me to more detailed plan making.

Jesus, we have confident hope in your care of us to enable Char to land a teaching position. May you be holding us in the palm of your hand!

TUESDAY, AUGUST 3, 1993

It was disappointing last evening to have so few show-ups. People balance so many things – get lost and forget. My mind wanders too – I'm only a stone's throw away from these folks. The money and job items are beginning to bother me. The ongoing focus to place our lives in the protective hold of your hands. To be utterly trusting – a real challenge.

WEDNESDAY, AUGUST 4, 1993

The thought struck: I write of the down-side of everything. The up-lifting of events of our lives go unnoticed. Jesus, during so fast a pace, aide me to recognize the beauty of your work in my life. Guide my day to be relaxed with an even measure of activity, slow-time and moments to feel of your care for me!

THURSDAY, AUGUST 5, 1993

It's mid-day! An easy paced AM. Worried about Char and MD and Insurance. Reading over old journal notes highlights the on-going problems and issues of life. Challenge really to enjoy the even-paced work load. Feel need to get moving to develop some process for enactment come September. Jesus, continue to be my inspiration!

With Char's birthday on August 8, we begin our yearly two-month birthday celebration. Between August and October 2, our family celebrates all our birthdays. I can see that char is heartbroken that we are here, and not there. It is a time that is all very hard on her.

She is not breathing as good as she could and the job search has been very energy consuming. I know that I still carry the grief of our Corpus Christi experience and this tells me it is doubly strong with her.

TUESDAY, AUGUST 31, 1993

End month 2! Our life is in your hands! Jesus, inspire, enable, make good our lives. Simplicity is an ideal I don't want to lose sight of as time goes by. We are forced to be such! Cleanse me of the wishful thinking that I continue to rest in. Thank you, Lord, for day One for the kids. Bless them in friendship making!

As the activity season in parish life gets underway, there is present in our lives an almost constant expression of our need to be held in the palm of Jesus' hands.

THURSDAY, SEPTEMBER 30, 1993

FULL MOON   Note in the lives of all! A cloudy morning. David's accident money will help a lot. What strikes me is that life gets larger as the kids get bigger. More is the name. This is something to be tired about. C.S. came to mind again yesterday – to what ifs! Jesus, keep on giving me the energy and need to be hopeful and faithful in all!

FRIDAY, OCTOBER 1, 1993

October is here – still hot! Called Herb in Yuma; he is always a word of encouragement and affirmation.

Yuma hangs over me as a real blessing that I walked from – not good or bad, just that I did it! As I end 52 years, I look ahead to further paths that will offer the feel of old, but the vigor of new.

MONDAY, OCTOBER 4, 1993

FRANCIS DAY A significant weekend! Birthday – like the yellow, gold, red Aspens! Beach Boys – Surprise! Old, and yet fresh, vital, and sparky. To keep the blood flowing is the key. Why was I so moody yesterday? As a new week begins, I look to new ideas, visions, etc. Jesus, lay your hand upon me, family, staff, all who come to my life this week.

The fall and winter of this year continued to be a time of many awkward feelings, events and on-going movement in the becoming a valued parish minister. Our family firms up to its presence through children's friends, work place involvements and general stability. Char began a teaching position at St. John's Indian Mission with 5-7 graders. It was a very new experience for her as well as an immersion into the Native American culture. Being 28 miles away, she left home very early and arrived back in early evening. But she loved it! Brian was on the high school golf squad. He played some of his best golf this year. Lynn bonded rather tightly with Melanie and they remained close for the next 10 years. David was an easy friend maker; he was accepted and thrived in the classroom as well as out of school.

The story of our/my heart is told in the journal notes for the remainder of the year.

WEDNESDAY, OCTOBER 13, 1993

A whole week has gone by without writing! Something wrong? I've failed? Taken a breather? Let other things take its place? Need a spark? Feelings I carry but cannot express, even in written form? Worries? Comfort? Jesus, spark me to feel my feelings and express them in some fashion!

THURSDAY, OCTOBER 14, 1993

Tired to start out! A long day ahead! A little hazy about positive outlook. What makes for all of this? Jesus, touch my heart and spirit through the people I meet today, some familiar, others brand new! I know you will, but that I may respond and see. Bless, Char!

FRIDAY, OCTOBER 15, 1993

"Broken Places" -- within more than without! Char's comment to me earlier, strikes a chord – for me, my insides are as valuable as my outside. What if outside is in poor shape? Going into this session after last night. Hard, but I hope to be as positive and untouched by whatever the numbers may be. Spirit of Excitement Come.

WEDNESDAY. OCTOBER 20, 1993

Days do slip by! Re-occurring thoughts of less-than and unsure, insecurity continue to touch me, hold me down. I so look to be settled – not in just money, but work, health, living. Why can't I be more self-giving.

Jesus, you know me inside and out. Prompt and guide me! Thank you for this day – I so want to trust!

FRIDAY, OCTOBER 22, 1993

Always attempting to find a way to make it money wise. How consuming and negative style. It just may be our claim at being poor. When the pressure lifts, I relax. Have much I depend on. Outside influences for good or bad sway me.

TUESDAY, OCTOBER 26, 1993

Strong doses of down – wondering where I am going and how. Char's job thing at St. John's breaks open – a relief – a challenge – Bless us Lord. Aid me to develop a positive attitude – to see the Spirit – excitement – urging me to new approaches!

THURSDAY, OCTOBER 28, 1993

A New approach – Jesus bless us in this effort – Char off to work and be for the Native children. Keep her safe. Give me hope and direction. Guide the car purchase plan! Be prudent – Be realistic – Be peaceful in all! Open my heart! So much to seek and ask, but to be powerless is significant. Allow.

SATURDAY, OCTOBER 30, 1993

How cute – every other day. Yesterday's meeting was life-giving and strong in vision. The next step is to follow through. That I may be instrumental in this – value-based work. Jesus be with Char in all things.

Guide us in our car work. I'm looking toward a peaceful day.

WEDNESDAY, NOVEMBER 3, 1993

Here I am in McDonald's at 35th Ave and Van Buren at 8:00 AM. A very strange life-style of coming, going and unsureness. Car issue is hard to resolve. Driving this little car is too challenging for me to long work with. Thoughts keep running in my head about all the what if's in our recent life. Jesus, allow for us!

FRIDAY, NOVEMBER 5, 1993

Another day! I hope – I trust – I resolve – I look for blessing in little things – with a real peaceful sense of Your care and presence. May I see you in words, gestures, persons and places. The disciplines I need, I must view as opening to grace.

TUESDAY, NOVEMBER 16, 1993

At Carl's – a long road to here! Though this AM – I need to cut out my own path for work. This may be dangerous, but it is most valuable. Some hints at being settled. This may fall apart, but I try to be positive and forward looking. Jesus be my guide and source of hope. Heal Char this day!

Chapter Nine

An Awkward Place

My journaling took a break between 1994 and 1997. This chapter includes memories, both good and bad, that I experienced through these years. In retrospect, I feel like I was the builder who did not prepare or examine, nor did I take stock of my position resources.

These four years embrace work and home transitions; I find that there is a constant blending occurring, influencing me and the family. Church ministry as I embraced it, and as Char and the kids observed it, continued to cost us all true discipleship.

At St. Andrew's, Fr. Joe and I started out on a very good footing. He invited me out to breakfast on a regular basis and willingly shared about the early beginning of St. Andrew's including the successes and problems with the former director of religious education. He was very candid.

Nearly every Friday afternoon Fr. Joe would stop into my office to talk about old times in the seminary, and the differences between Phoenix and Cleveland regarding priestly ministry. Occasionally, we would get into my work, especially the RCIA. I felt that he valued my presence and I could tell our family life was of interest to him. He accented the family as the church of the Home and we were all encouraged by him. This timeframe was very much a honeymoon time at St. Andrew's.

I felt full of ideas for the Catechumenate. Yet, Fr. Joe didn't understand why I saw changes to be important. The chief example of this was the Easter Vigil celebration of that first year. When I worked with Fr. Richard in Yuma, I was used to making plans and then working hard carrying them out independently. Unlike Fr. Richard, Fr. Joe was not as liturgically progressive. I created my plan and presented it to him about 3 weeks ahead of Holy Week. He never brought it up and we never discussed it. This, it turns out, was a mistake. I took his silence as approval. He never approached me about it, so I figured all was good.

About one hour before the Liturgy for Easter Vigil began, Fr. Joe came and asked if anything would be different than last year.

I was astonished. At that moment, I realized he had not even looked at my notes! I gave him a fresh copy right then. He had many questions concerning the changes being initiated and worked hard to follow my plan. But from time to time throughout, he launched out on his own during the ceremonies.

As the first year ended, Fr. Joe and I formally met. We both expressed a positive outlook to continue for a second year. All that was said about the Easter Vigil debacle was some vague comment from him that I needed to clarify new ideas with him more regularly. And that, was that. I did not sign any agreement or review.

The summer brought two new staff on board, a surprise to me as there was no discussion about any of it at our staff meetings. In contrast, when I was hired, there was a very open gathering and the entire staff was involved in the process to give their blessing of the decision. The pastor had invited two women. Both were named Mary. One Mary was hired as Director of Children's' Religious Education and the other Mary would be Director of Liturgy and Music. Both were professionally trained.

Fr. Joe also launched another major move: a major building project. Our quickly growing parish needed a Church, and additional meeting rooms and classrooms. This effort proved to be a great distraction in the parish life. Those of us involved with Formation, kept our focus and proceeded.

The second year became a lot busier with evening programs and planning meetings. I knew this would be the case, but it remains a drain on family life. Brian and Lynn were now teenagers with interests, needs, and maturity that was forming them into young adults.

Char found a teaching position at a new charter school in northwest Phoenix, a drive across town. Her salary was an excellent addition to our bottom line.

Brian had his best season of golf during this school year. It was also a time that he gained interest in making friends with popular guys and was developing friendships with girls. Enter the disquieting time of teen-life!

Lynn and her friend Melanie became fast friends with the two Mary's on the staff. They taught preschool religious education in place of attending classes themselves. What operators! And David made friends with neighborhood boys, but, found himself getting into some trouble due to free-spirited parental guidance. All of this surely expanded my grasp of parenting and the lofty calling Char and I attempted to respond to and live.

In late 1994, early 1995 Char's asthma took a turn for the worse. She then had a seriously dangerous reaction to the steroids she had to take. After a week, she was back to the classroom of 2nd graders.

I conceived a modified use of the parish renewal process, RENEW, as a freestanding project for Lent in fulfillment of my role of Adult Formation Director. Designed to be offered during the six weeks of Lent, I pieced together the combination of Scripture, Reflection, Teaching and Discussion for the six weeks of Lent. I recruited a small team to compose the content for each week to attract participants and to handle the logistics involved in planning the variety of times and places at Church to carry this off.

I was careful to let the pastor know about each step of the program, allowing him to review the plans of the sessions. But, as we started it, parishioners occasionally would ask Fr. Joe questions. We did not brief him as we didn't think he needed to bother himself with some of these details. When he did not have an answer to these questions, he grew upset and rattled.

Unfortunately, this put me in a bad place. He believed or considered that I was leading a conspiracy against him! And so, about the middle/end of March, he came over to my office, came in, closed the door and sat down. All very unusual for him. He merely said that he has other plans for adult formation, and I am not invited back for next year. I asked why and he had no real response. He got up and left.

Now, I worked at two successive parishes and was fired from both. I became frightened, enraged, confused. I went to the library where it was dark and quiet and found myself pulling the intercom phone out of the wall in retaliation--an unusual reaction to an unusual situation once again. I must be becoming a failure at this parish type of ministry and work. My confidence quickly left me. I went home and didn't return for three days.

For all the sophistication of the parish's size and success in 1995, I believe Fr. Joe's dysfunction as a pastoral administrator was now evident. Nothing more was ever said to me again until early June. Fortunately, the Liturgy Director took over the Easter Vigil Ceremony planning. I only had to meet with her several times. I often thought, so much for Fr. Joes' Church of the Home!

How hard it was to tell Char and the kids. I'm sure that they saw this as another punch in the gut given to them by the Church.

Sadly, no parishes were advertising for professional Formation Directors. Instead, I began seeking out supermarket stocking jobs and I was overqualified!

In early June, I finished up at St. Andrew Church, moved out of my office, and decided I would take a week at home before turning up the effort to find work.

So much uncertainty. Should I continue in Church Ministry? Do we move out of town again! What about Char? What should she do as she was also seeking a new position. We had far more questions than answers.

Chapter Ten

The Resurrection Morning

I was washing the living room walls when I took a breather and settled down with the Sunday paper classified ads. Under Employment Opportunities, I saw the Catholic Diocese of Phoenix needed a Coordinator of Christian Formation to travel in the counties of Northern Arizona. I read it two more times to really understand it and then I sent a letter of interest and my resume. "By the Grace of God." It was now late June, a few weeks after leaving St. Andrew's.

I contacted John, the Director of Catechesis for the Diocese, after the Fourth of July. He only knew that such a position was under discussion and was not aware of the ad. I waited and waited, but there were no calls in July. Then in early August, Fr. John calls to invite me to have lunch with him the following week. Wow! Fr. John is the pro-tem Director of the department of Christian Formation and I was meeting him the following Tuesday.

We sat down in an Asian Restaurant and he asked me to share a little about my background. I talked throughout lunch. Soon, he told me that this position would be both an extension of the catechetical offices' service to parishes as well as a PR effort. The goal for the person filling this role would be to knit together relationships between the diocesan offices and the parishes and missions in northern Arizona!

I asked what the next step in the process would be and learned this meeting was all there would be. He then told me that I was hired! Wow! Again!

On the 20th of August, I was off to Sedona with Fr. John, John from the Catechetical office, and the youth minister for the diocese to meet with the three vicars of the northern counties. These three priests, all knowledgeable of the inner workings of the Diocese, were concerned that I was being sent to their areas to overreach and to police their parishes for the central office. Fr. John and John from the office of Catechesis stressed that my role was to be one of service to the parishes, especially in catechetical formation, plus offer any other resources to be helpful. My priesthood background, combined with my work in Yuma were very positive elements that clinched this position for me.

The traveling involved in the position would soon be revealed as the biggest challenge I would need to adapt to. Many times, I would drive 600 to 800 miles in one single day. The adjustment would also be difficult for my family especially when I would need to be away overnight. Brian, a junior in high school, found my absence to be especially difficult although he never shared that directly with me. I only found this out much later from a girlfriend he was dating at the time. My absence was a shock to his system!

Coordinator of Christian Formation for Northern Arizona was my new title and there would be 19 parishes and missions for me to visit on regularly.

Generally, I found the pastors to be welcoming and I even struck up a friendship with most of them. There was one pastor, an older man who had been very involved in the Phoenix area as the founding pastor of a good size community. When Fr. Jim became ill, the bishop invited him to minister at a beautiful community in Camp Verde, Arizona. A valley-like area in the mountains that rise from the Phoenix valley, leading to Sedona and Flagstaff, Arizona, Camp Verde was lovely. However, it was lost on Fr. Jim who felt that the Bishop was putting him out to pasture.

The first time I called Fr. Jim to set up an appointment to introduce myself, he refused, saying he was too busy. I explained that my visit would be for only 15 minutes and that I merely wished to get acquainted. Finally, he agreed to see me at about 9:15 AM, meaning I would need to leave home no later than 7:30 AM--in the heart of the rush-hour--to drive through the center of Phoenix to make the hour and a half trip in time.

On the phone, the wary pastor made clear to me that he could spend only 15 minutes with me. He had other matters to attend to that morning and I assured him that I would only take a few minutes out of his schedule. When I arrived just at 9:15, he answered the doorbell. Upon his lead, I followed him back to the private area of the rectory to his residence. The television was broadcasting the O.J. Simpson trial and right then, I realized his "important other matters" was that the verdict to the trial was to be announced in 15 minutes.

Right then, I told him that I too had been following the case on TV and would welcome watching the verdict announcement along with him.

Great!

We sat and watched it together for about an hour, sharing our OJ thoughts, insights, and opinions. An hour and 15 minutes later, Fr. Jim turns to me and wants to know what he could do for me.

That's when I shared with him my mission and that was to be of help. The Bishop's office had not sent me to spy on him but to support him. I shared my priestly ministry, years in religious education work, and about my current family's life, when he asked about my experience and background. Soon, as I talked, I could see him relax, and then he began to tell his story. At about 11:00, he asked if I would like to see the church and then join him for lunch. It was 1:30 pm before I left Fr. Jim. My 15-minute visit had turned into a full morning and part of an afternoon. What's more, we began a friendship that day that I cherished for the rest of my years working in the Diocese.

Turns out, I was instrumental in peeling back some layers of discontent, according to some co-workers at the Diocesan Center. My liaison with Fr. Jim helped him open up to viewing the downtown Phoenix office a little differently, more positively.

Driving became an adventure in its own right. For two years, in fulfilling this role, I figured I drove 18,000 miles each year in my own little Ford Escort!

Reflecting on those days, I'm not sure it was built for the mountainous roads that were involved in these trips. On my very first, trip the battery went dead in the driveway of St. Francis of Assisi church in Bagdad, AZ. This tiny company town, dedicated to the copper mining industry, was nestled in an isolated valley of northwestern Arizona.

On another adventurous trip, I was off to Kingman, AZ, a town located about 150 miles northwest, about an hour outside of Las Vegas, NV. Route 93, the only route between Phoenix and Las Vegas was a dangerous road. On that fresh September morning, it was a pleasure to meet I-40, the interstate that replaced Route 66 in the Southwest. I was about to exit the highway when the Escort stopped running. I coasted off the road and came to a stop at the end of the exit. Keep in mind, this transpired before cell phones were a frequent tool in 1995!! I locked the car and walked to a gas station where I called the parish in Kingman, St. Mary. Soon, I reached a towing service and had the car towed to the gas station only to learn that the serpentine belt had broken. A two-day, $250 prospect, replacing the belt would consume all my $650 monthly auto use advancement. Imagine my relief when I called the downtown office only to be reassured by Fr. Long's assistant that I would be reimbursed for this issue and still receive the advance.

I found St. Mary's to be a wonderful place to stay overnight. It was a cross-roads location with a young pastor – Fr. Jim. I often used their facilities for meeting and workshops in the north; the hospitality was always great. I became good friends with the parish staff!

I was surprised to be instantly accepted by the diocesan ministry of nearly 100 personnel of the Diocesan Center. As the first few months went by, I was being asked by Sr. Mary Ann, the Chancellor, and by Bishop O'Brien about "news" from the north. They were interested in how a few specific priests were receiving my help and my visits. Answering with diplomacy, I was always honored to be asked, yet careful about what I reported. Never would I allow my role to be merely a reporting one, as a watchdog. At Christmas time of the first year, I sat with Sr. Mary Ann for an hour or more, as she highlighted several wider issues that would impact the central offices' ministry in the northern portion of the diocese.

She shared the need for the consolidation of parishes in some areas and greater development of parishes in other communities. How and when this would happen was the question.

As the second half of my first year matured, I found that the Catechetical Ministry Office looked to me to strengthen their training of parish catechists and develop ministry leaders in the north. I met with John and his associate, Carol, to organize our approach in these outlying parishes. It was then I began meeting monthly with the already established Leaders of the Catechetical Ministry Board. Since I already stayed overnight often, these sessions were in evenings or early morning to accommodate better participation of parishes.

Realizing Saturdays and Sundays were better days to meet with a wider group, I began to expand my week of traveling. Char and the family did not welcome my choices although the communities I was ministering welcomed the weekend hours.

This leads me to another situation that was, for me, both a challenge and a clear positive opportunity. I was attempting to cover a good measure of the parishes with some modest introduction to catechist training. Some parish directors were great at this and other communities fell short. My plan was to have the larger, more self-sufficient parish sponsor training. I centered my teaching at the host parish and to those catechists who didn't have trained leaders in their small communities. The parish in Bullhead City, AZ hosted such a gathering on a Saturday morning. St. Margaret Mary parish had a pastor about my age. Our conversations often went to our seminary days and the differing styles of priestly ministry that had evolved over the years. Fr. Peter presented himself as a more conservative Church leader. He watched carefully, that there was not "off-the-cuff" teaching that might confuse parishioners.

I decided to take my "road-show" to St. Margaret Mary Parish. I arrived there in late afternoon on Friday. Fr. Peter welcomed me with usual gracious hospitality. We had dinner together at a Casino across the Colorado River in Laughlin, Nevada. He usually retired rather early leaving me with the T.V. or reading. This evening I spent some time with my notes for the next day.

Fr. Peter told me he wanted to sit in on the early portion of my presentation. My topic was "Social Justice in the Church Today." I went to bed about 10:00 PM with the plan to wake about 6:30 AM. I awakened about 4-4:30 to the pleasant aroma of bread baking and muffins from scratch. Fr. had told me when we first met that he baked on Saturdays. It still took me by surprise this morning. After I enjoyed my muffins and coffee, I headed to the parish hall to set up for the 9:00 session. Again, to my surprise, parish women laid out coffee and breakfast cakes for the guests coming to class.

I started on time with a "prayer experience" and began to move into my outline. Just about then, Fr. Peter slipped into the back of the room. I paused and invited him to join a table group. He did so and became a part of group discussion as the morning went by. At the break-time, he came to me to compliment me on the variety of content and the abundance of notes I provided. He excused himself due to a previous appointment.

About 10 minutes later the rather new parish religious education director came in to merely "observe me". Pat was trained at a conservative Catholic College in the eastern United States. She wasn't exactly a friend of the diocese's brand of religious education, both in methodology and content. She said nothing to me when the morning was over. I packed up and left. I guess that "a good time was had by all." I traveled back to Phoenix and home through Kingman and route 93 to Wickenburg, AZ. This town prides itself as a true "wild west" cowboy town.

Well, on this Saturday afternoon they celebrated their rodeo with a parade through town. This event closed all incoming traffic on the road I was on and I didn't know of this until I was in the parking-lot style of traffic. There was no other way to go! The usual 4½ hour trip home took nearly 7 hours.

The family aspect of all this can be summed up by telling that Char was alone at home when I arrived about 7:00 pm. The kids were out. Brian had a date, Lynn was staying at Mel's, and David was at a sleep-over. None of them liked my absence when they figured I should be home. All was forgiven and forgotten when we went out for Sunday dinner, a recently adopted tradition of eating out as a family on Sunday Afternoons.

My relationships began to mature with the other staff persons in the Department of Christian Formation. About mid-way through my first year, Sr. Dolorette became the director. She and I hit it off very quickly. Sr. Dolorette saw the value of my work and role, both for the department and for the diocese. She was thoughtful, always inquiring of the health of my family, each time asking about everyone by name and offering support to me as a family man. She was very clear in directing me to make up the time I was away at night and on weekends. In the office, I received a small area in the secretary section that was my desk when I was in town.

I found myself ever more relating to John and Carol in the office of Catechetical Ministry.

Gradually, I made their mission mine involving myself in the work of the Diocese in the north. John came to me one day and asked if I wish to join him and Carol at the national conference of catechetical leaders to be held in Detroit, MI.

He had received Sister D's approval and his office would handle all costs. I saw this opportunity as an offer I could not refuse. With the support of them both, I felt very affirmed in this situation.

Sr. Dolorette's secretary and the department office manager, made it clear to the secretary's that I was on equal footing with the other directors. I did not have a secretary and so my work was treated as any director. She also made sure that all understood I was a full-time staff person even though I was away so often.

The Diocesan Center's old building was at capacity. They became hallowed halls as the years went by and haunting stories were common. When I came and went from the second-floor, I used the exit door next to the Bishop's office. As I would pass his door, he would often ask me about my travels and about certain priests, whose parishes were of interest to him. In the second year, the three churches in the city of Flagstaff, fell into this category. Rumors were turning into facts that St. Pius the Tenth, Our Lady of Guadalupe, and Nativity needed to be consolidated into one location with a different name. How, when, where and who, were looming, major questions. When I was asked about my thoughts concerning such a plan change, I couldn't honestly answer.

I had not been a part of the discussion and I really didn't know the problems well enough.

Similarly, pastors experiencing problems, whether personal, professional, parish-related, financials, or otherwise, often approached me for my counsel. It was natural for them to pick my brain as I represented the Diocese. I wanted to be helpful, yet I had to be very careful not to get into the middle of anything.

St. Joseph Church in Williams, AZ was pastored by a priest who was not very old, yet who had some major illnesses. The parish wasn't too large but was very conservatively-oriented and Father was very careful to keep all things personal and relative to the parish, low and under the radar. Bishop O'Brien asked me if I knew the pastor and I answered that I only sat with him once. I learned he had been unable to make a contact with the pastor and asked me to follow up personally. Father was very ill, was moving very slowly, and had been visiting with family out of town. I reported this to Bishop, who realized the sick priest had been avoiding the Bishop as he knew that he could not continue much longer in this way. After a few more months Father was reassigned to sick leave. The parish was covered by the priests in Flagstaff and then a deacon was assigned as administrator.

As I continued into the second year, I managed to piece together a ministry day for all the various parish volunteers involved in Christian Formation. I invited all the directors of Christian Formation to lead one or two workshops in their area of expertise.

They were very generous with their time in visiting Lake Havasu City, AZ and Our Lady of the Lake, about a 150-mile trip from Phoenix. The parish had just completed a large parish hall with about 12 classrooms and a kitchen. It was an ideal place for such a workshop experience and the parish staff was very hospitable. There were 150 ministers who attended. They positively received the ministry day. I felt very good about this accomplishment.

When I began ministry in northern Arizona, Fr. John and then Sr. Dolorette asked me to prepare a weekly report about my travels and various experiences. I found out that my position was an experiment. So far, I was successful.

In late spring of 1997, Sr. Dolorette met with me for my yearly work evaluation. Rather than the typical review format, Sr. Dolorette prompted me to do a self-study and a self-appreciation of the ministry I was doing. She was interested in the practical successes of my work as well as the spiritual. And as always, she would ask how my family life was affected.

When we were through, she asked if she could speak to me about something else. There was another position in the department she was thinking about me to fill and wanted to know if I would be interested. It seems a conversation had begun at the Bishop's administrative board to reestablish the Family Life Office. I responded with several questions about what type of major work the office and me would be responsible for. Why did it close some eight years earlier?

Who was the director? I had many questions and she had so few answers. The position and plan had not even been approved! Sr. Dolorette explained that this should happen in the next two or three months, or early July. The position would be widely advertised and then, all the qualified candidates, interviewed. Sister explained that I would have my foot in the door, since I was already a part of the department, and I am known by many in the diocese. I threw my hat in the ring.

The following week, Sister Dolorette sent to me a vast array of printed material from the records of the earlier office. I took the next two days at home to read and ponder, commenting, highlighting portions, and asking questions. When I returned to the office, Sr. Dolorette and I sat for a lengthy time while I outlined my interest, my fears, and my goals in accepting this position if it were to be offered to me. She did share some history in detailing the terrible status this position was in when the priest counsel and the Bishop dissolved it in 1992. She highlighted that at the beginning, half of my job would be to embrace a strong stance of the offices' importance in the overall ministry of the Diocese. She accented that my easy-going, softer side could be a hazard to this situation.

Still more growth ahead? It would be a few months before I would have more answers.

Chapter Eleven

A Minor Prophecy Fulfilled

In the summer days of 1997, I traveled much less. Over the next weeks, I watched as the Family Life Office position was advertised, and several interviews, carried out. The Bishop's Board finalized the full establishment of the office. Finally, in early August, Sr. Dolorette called me into her office and offered the position to me. I accepted it and she proceeded to arrange a start date and the process of announcement to the Diocese at large.

On September 1, exactly two years after I began as Coordinator of Formation in Northern Arizona, I opened the Office of Family Life as Director. We turn another page!

Back in Yuma, some 15 years earlier, Fr. Nacho, the youthful associate pastor, told me that someday I would land in a Diocesan Office position.

"Here I am! Thanks, Father."

This summer goes down in our family's history as bittersweet. Both Char and I were hired into new positions. Char became Director of Formation at St. Benedict Church in Chandler, AZ and I began my new duties. Char's asthma had worsened and breathing had become very difficult for her. She ended up in the hospital with an asthma-induced heart attack. Fr. Pat, the pastor at St. Benedict, visited her often in the hospital and at home. He began to question her ability to take on her position.

Another miracle! Char was convinced of her abilities and strength and even began to write a plan of action to invite and prepare catechists. On September 1, she, too, began her work at St. Benedict Church. We are off and running. The children were happy as well – they know where Mom and Dad were every day!

The secretary registered me to attend the National conference of Family Life Directors in Boca Raton, FL in late September. The day before I left, I received a message from Bishop O'Brien's secretary inviting me to have lunch with Bishop on Thursday, the first day of the Conference. The surprises keep coming! I find out that he is the chairman of the Family Life committee for the NCCB and will be the opening speaker at the conference.

I met Bishop O'Brien in the lobby of the conference hotel as arranged. After we ordered our meals, the Bishop congratulated me on my new position in the Diocese. He then revealed several pastors who did not believe I was the right person for the position. They would be watching me closely. Even more, they did not fully support reopening that office. My major task will be to begin to discover parish needs and to offer service in a specific area of ministry. Bishop O'Brien's personal objective was to see significantly greater improvement to marriage preparation! He asked me to devise a plan of action with a two-month timeline and prepare to present it to both the Priest and the diocesan Pastoral Councils.

I was disappointed to learn the Conference was less than impressive! I did not find it as an opportunity to learn much. I judge meetings like this, by the style and spirit of the Liturgy planning. And, unfortunately, the 300 persons came all the way from around the country did not equate to a prayerful community. All in all, I'm still glad I went.

Returning to mounds of paperwork, I began to plan to meet boards and committees from various areas that came under the direction of Family Life Ministry. With the consultation of the Family Life board, I zeroed my attention and effort to the whole area of Marriage Preparation.

A pre-marriage couples' committee was assembled. The committee's mission was to quickly outline a simple operation process that would prepare couples in the greater Phoenix area for marriage. The Engagement Experience was designed for Friday evening and all-day Saturday sessions offered to various parishes. We planned to begin in 1998.

In the remaining weeks of 1997, I sat in on the Engagement Encounter, the Natural Family Planning board meeting, the Marriage Encounter, and yes, both the Priest Board and the Pastoral council. With The Engagement Experience on the horizon, within a brief timeline, I had pulled it off with the help of the committee; there was little these watchful groups could find to criticize.

As the new department director, I found the staff to be very supportive. Directed by Sr. Dolorette's secretary, there was much print-work to produce for the "program" as I came to call The Engagement Experience. In the spring of 1998, the chairperson of Engaged Encounter called me very upset. She wanted to speak with me about our two programs surviving. I met her, a nurse supervisor used to calling the shots in her world, at St. Joseph Hospital dining hall for lunch. She was insulted believing that our "program" stole the initials of Engaged

Encounter, "EE". Doing my best to reassure that we had no intention of damaging her programming.

Despite my best efforts to encourage her that both programs could thrive in the growing Diocese of Phoenix, she did not believe her program was endorsed by the Diocese and informed me that they will discontinue their program at the end of the year.

I reported this, my first minor setback as the office director, to Sr. Dolorette. Within a few weeks, I learned from her that the Bishop was dissatisfied with what he had heard about Engaged Encounter; he was not bothered to hear they were closing.

The "Program" consumed a lot of my time and energy in the first year. We held the traveling road show in various parish halls around the Phoenix area. I would roll in, set up, serve, and provide all supplies as the leader of the session, an emcee-type. The end of 1998 brought a series of rapid-fire events that cost me dearly in mind, body and spirit! In mid-September, I went to San Antonio for the National Conference of Family Life Directors, and then I followed up beginning early October with a Program. In mid-month, I arranged for a diocesan-wide marriage minister training day. I invited a guest from the Diocese of Omaha to present a day of instruction on an Engaged Couple dynamic called FOCCUS.

On Sunday of that same weekend, I was responsible for the arrangement of tables and chairs at an outdoor rally sponsored by an inter-faith committee that I was on to promote family strength in an urban environment.

Then, on Friday morning, I developed chest pains that wouldn't go away. I was 58, overweight, and I was stressed by work as well as worried about our youth-filled family. I asked Char to call 911. They came and took me to the hospital with them.

It took about three blood draws and 12 hours for the medical staff to conclude that I had a serious heart attack. I was transferred to another hospital four days later where I found out that I had three serious blockages requiring immediate open-heart surgery.

Brian, our oldest child, expressed his worry, "How many of these have you done?" When Dr. Darrell Stein answered, "About 1,000," I could see Brian's' relief on his face. Dr. Stein got down on his knees to speak clearly, caringly, and directly to me, face to face. God was telling me about the healing work he planned to do tomorrow. Dr. Stein explained he would hold my heart, repair three arteries, and then put me back together. The Lord bent over and cared for me. After five hours and, then several more hours, I remember Char and Lynn standing at the foot of my bed.

O Holy Night!

The period of recovery lasted about nine weeks. This period was filled with emotions, moods, limitations, and refreshing newness. I began to recognize myself anew, feeling as a new person in our home. My roles at home and at work had changed. At work, I had to hire a person to handle all the good service work. Soon, I called upon the advisory board to assist in decisions I had to make and found it to be a great help.

Finally, in 1998, I helped as best I could at the final Engagement Experience for the year. I was hopeful that I would have an assistant in time for the February program. I was excused from work for the first two hours of the days I had cardiac rehab, three times a week for twelve weeks.

A busy year ends, a busy year begins.

As the months moved forward, the year became a banner for all of us. I grew stronger in my continued recovery from heart surgery, Char was taking improved medication to treat her asthma, and our children and entire family, experienced guarded growth in wisdom, age, and grace.

It had been 25 years since that autumn evening in the living room when we had married on November 7th of 1974. We wanted to celebrate the anniversary with the renewal of our wedding vows along with the worshiping community at St. Benedict. In the afternoon, we took family photos and relaxed until we went to the Italian bistro where David bussed tables for a splendid meal together. There was a pretty clear addition to our family with the entry of Dwight, Lynn's recent boyfriend. He worked hard to blend with this rather progressive Catholic family.

At 22, Dwight's three-year age advantage over Lynn came with far more adult experiences than Lynn had had. Through friends he gained knowledge of Jesus and became very devoted to Christian living. Dwight was attending a non-denominational church in Gilbert yet since meeting Lynn, he joined us to worship at Mass in St. Benedict Church.

My journal entries are much more family centered, than they were five years ago. I believe the time I had spent away from home, traveling for the diocese, was something that the boys, especially did not manage too well. Lynn, however, became very close to Melanie's family and began to be a catechist (religion teacher) for Char. This and her work kept her busy, and not feel so apart from me.

As I matured in the Family Life Office position, I found myself gaining acceptance by my peers in the Formation Department as well as by other diocesan leaders. This was surely a confidence booster for me.

To prepare for this section of my life and ministry, I asked a good friend, Peter, for some feedback concerning his impressions of me and my style of workmanship.

Peter's insights at that time were:

--Richard is a confident and rather laid-back individual. He is a great listener who solicits opinions and brings people together. He honors and empowers their suggestions.

--Richard is very open showing a desire to be inclusive, not divisive. He quickly wins the trust of others making him an effective leader.

--Did Richard show frustrations? He was not impressed with the qualities of the new Bishop, finding their differences a means of making their relationship tense. This never was shown publicly in any of his classes or ministries. It was a personal cross for Richard.

THURSDAY, JANUARY 13, 2000

In the morning! A speaking engagement. It's good to be accepted, praised and appreciated. How powerful is the recognition of the gift to speak well and read well. Thank you, Lord! I feel very much as Samuel. The Lord calls and speaks. The message is sent. I receive it, accept it, embrace it, let it become bone and flesh of me. Then, I must give the gift that I've been given.

It's at this time that priestly ministry still pulls, and the yearning opens wounds. I feel graced that I'm going to Cleveland next month. Bless Nick in his living, healing, and his viewing of life – counter his depression.

FRIDAY, JANUARY 14, 2000

TGIF With these nights out, the week gets long. I begin today with the hope of getting and keeping all my pegs in order.

The old feast of St. Hilary! Those were the days, my friend. But, not the days to relive -- get caught up in -- settle there! But too, they were the beginning of care, love, interest with Char. Days of passion for retreat work and outreach care. Days to lead, grow, appreciate, and recognize gifts. Days of friendships and grace! Thank you, Jesus for this time of life! "The Swinger" priest – 25 years – 30 years!

We move on! Jesus, you love me, care for me!

It was an exciting time as we are building a house! A Grand Slam! My blood pressure continues to worry me and I found myself needing some advice assurance, warning, something to settle on. What's more, I have a hard time balancing my diet. Discipline comes in many forms. With high blood pressure and high cholesterol, I am constantly taking pills, pills, and more pills.

Weighing the future, I consider going natural but am concerned about the results now.

I try to focus on relaxing more, eating better, and learning NOT TO WORRY!

SATURDAY, JANUARY 22, 2000

I have given myself to Char. Her beauty, spirit, values and grace continue to shade my person. This is a fantastic experience. Over the years I have grown, matured, become freer and more spontaneous do to this phenomenon! There is a zest for life that is preserved in her and I'm picking up its waves. This has contributed to the overall betterment of my life. Today, for instance, Char highlights the value of a "do-nothing" day. Well, I've taken hold of that – only went shopping, went to Home Depot, will be going to L.A. Fitness.

Even though I was working more and assuming greater responsibilities in this director position, I found that an age-old problem surfaced in my life. I was gaining weight! A few ounces became a few pounds, became 10-15 pounds. When I took my blood pressure it was not borderline high and I walked almost daily for one-half hour. But, the sweet roll at breakfast, the sweet latte at lunchtime and the heavy dinners and pie in the evening, solidly overcame my resolutions, careful lists and many books I had on diets. The weight I had lost around the heart surgery time had returned and then some.

I continued to bounce around, trying to lose on my own until I went into a Weight Watcher center and talked with a coach.

She easily convinced me to buy into the process and work the program. For many years, I was sure that losing weight was 90% mental effort. I signed in and began meeting attendance and weigh-in the next Monday after work. It was a dedicated hour of my life until I came down about 25 pounds. My mind was in the right place! It only took me about six months to reach my goal weight.

At this early point of 2000, I realized that working until we were 65 years old was financially, a necessity. Char and I also agreed that we would not rule out going to age 70, health permitting.

Diocesan Ministry Update, My Family Life and Me

Toward the end of 1999, I hired a woman to help handle the buying, hauling, and arrangement of supplies and snacks, and to assist the caterer at serving breakfast and lunch. Such a helper changed my whole mindset regarding the Program. All of this shifted the Engagement program into high-gear, I could now concentrate much more on the team of presenters.

As I worked with and met with the team, they offered suggestions that proved very helpful to the maturing of the project. Our Engagement Experience had settled into a good rhythm and its success was proven.

Chapter Twelve

Family Visits and Back to Ministry

In February 2000, I took a vacation week to return to Ohio and Erie, PA for a visit. My older brother Eugene had been ill, had had surgery, and was slow at recuperation. I left on leap day, Feb. 29, with plans to return home on March 6.

TUESDAY, FEBRUARY 29, 2000

Well, I'm off into the wild blue yonder! I left behind a son that won't greet me and a son who has a whole life of challenge ahead! I prayed Lynn and Char would be strong, care for one another, and that David may bring the peace that he preaches. For me, I go to visit, to be supportive, to accent wholeness, health and brotherliness. I wondered of the hopes and stress of aging.

Jesus, I set myself before you on this journey of miles, heart, head and time. Hold me up. Keep me healthy. Inspire me to take care of myself.

WEDNESDAY, MARCH 1, 2000

I'm here! It is early morning. Yesterday, it was sunny and comfortable and today, at this early hour, it is rainy and very wintry looking.

I'm a little nervous about seeing Nick and Rose, about getting around, and about the endless busyness that this time will take become. I need to remember the words of Cardinal Bernadine – " the person in front of you is the most important and only one at this time". The prayer for them is attention and that Jesus will be my guide in all of this. Bless my family. Bless Rose and Nick – may our time be healing, loving, uplifting for him/for us.

And...may I get a cheap car that will take me!

THURSDAY, MARCH 2, 2000

Yesterday was special. Got a car – no problem. I saw Jean and Len, Len's parents. Aging is a wondrous adventure -- there are many downs and some ups! Jean has done it very gracefully --Len is very limited. Rose goes on -- very same. Nick is not as bad looking and acting as I thought. Fortunately, I wasn't boiled over. The biggest setback of the day was Len. He looked drawn and worn and very thin. Yet, he says he has only lost 6 pounds. He sounds very negative. More than usual. He has poor work – paint factory! He should write a book. I really feel for him. I am reminded that I have nothing to complain about in the face of his instability!

SUNDAY, MARCH 5, 2000

Mid-morning – been to church, out to eat, relaxing. Mass was very eastern, non-committal and without a strong life. We have a gift in our manner of celebration that is wonderful and to be grateful for! I'm missing home now.

I wait to return with a fresh sense of getting on board. This week will be full until the surgery, and then, very different. I've been immersed in family and old friends. I feel very blest; I've been able to set aside the home troubles and step-parent. They won't change, but hopefully, I have, and I'll be able to live with them in a better fashion.

Protect me in my journey back. May Barb and Len be peaceful in my being there. Heal their hearts and free them of burdens that are theirs

MONDAY, MARCH 6, 2000

Yesterday – a long generous day. I felt good about being with Jan and Ernie, and very blessed to be with Barb and Len and family. So very nice are Jake and Larrissa. My heart goes out to Len. I wish that – I pray that something comes to light for him. I don't know how discouraged I'd be if I had his plight. Topping off the day was speaking with Char. Distance does make the heart grow fonder and yearn more. The one you love becomes the center of attention as the days go by. How hard it will be – the two hours that I'm home and she isn't tonight. Bless me Jesus, as I enter back into reality – family, work, etc. health with surgery attached!

As I left Ohio, I was struck with the reality, we are all older in age, but with that comes the charge of illness, slowness of thought and greater interest in establishing our legacy. What we'll be remembered for by our families. This train of thought is not bad or selfish. It is what the last third of life is about!

I no sooner settled into work and the home-life activities that I was scheduled for gall-bladder removal surgery. I went into the hospital understanding that I would be there about two days and then have about four days at home.

The desert in our lives is the place where in our poverty, our sin, our pain and in our need, we come to know the Lord.   **--Maria Boulding**

Well, the time of recuperation spread out a little.

THURSDAY, MARCH 16, 2000

The back to work day! I'm excited about getting back to it! It's been a gentle and yet a very good progression to recovery. I'm peaceful, in good spirits, and feel ready. Rest is Wonderful.

I'm pleased that I discovered a social/justice approach to a prayer-time for Saturday. Arizona hunger and poverty. Jesus, my thoughts are bland now. The issues are not alarming. I'm rested, I guess. Instill in me a clear vision of work, life, relationship. May I truly grasp the "one thing that matters."

In April I begin to rise out of some self-defeating thought and recognize how utterly dependent I am upon the Lord.

SUNDAY, APRIL 9, 2000

Fifth Sunday of Lent

Early evening. It even crossed my mind today to put this away until I really miss it and go after it. But, I'm not there yet. It's been a quiet day.

When I went to the Fitness Center, I weighed more -- 169 ½, and that's bad! I am not watching, caring, loving myself! Perhaps, as I look out at all the issues – I fail to really respect myself. Weight, exercise, look at my inner self, prayer, these are the values I should embrace. I enter into this old Passiontide with this in mind and in heart, and with will and sincere hope. A daily resolve will be my path. Jesus, hold me up in this little effort. Self-regard is significantly important.

MONDAY, APRIL 10, 2000

Today has been good. Busy, some frustration, reflective at times. I find out that Brian is pretty laid back. I live in hope that he is cleaning up. The little group of them don't have it easy. No power is a big order! I await David's anger over no lunch money. My resolves are holding for the day. One of them at a time. Jesus, give me on-going peace. Bless Char in health and work and spirit as we move on! Bless our meeting tomorrow with Bishop O'Brien.

TUESDAY, APRIL 11, 2000

Early evening! A day of talking. Value? Where do we go? We must determine this. Not really uplifting for me! A radical change is needed – business cannot be as usual. This goes for me personally. And, I don't have any answers either – even for myself. What can I change? Regarding work, home, activities, care for self, family life, Char and me.

FRIDAY, APRIL 14, 2000

Resolves go down the tube! Yet, I am staying with the watchful eye on the eating thing. The Seder Meal was very good – light, yet of meaning and substance in the reflection on the Eucharist. I am grateful for the energy to carry it out and how well all seemed to work. Jesus Bless this day of peace and justice!

Be with David.

SUNDAY, APRIL 16, 2000

PASSION/PALM SUNDAY

Here is the Week of Weeks! I read of the word passion" with passion" – the thrill, the excitement, the sensible fever in any action. But, with this comes the giving, the sacrifice, the letting go, the dying. This we celebrate this week. How pivotal a departing point in terms of my/our life. I'm having pain that I don't really know why. LITTLE IS AS I WOULD LIKE IT!

Char and I are in a good place – may we be strong, faithful and wise in all we say and do. May hugging, kissing, deep affection stir us to ongoing oneness. We walk in passion together!

Jesus, give each day this week a special flare! A point of significance to more deeply appreciate your love and to recognize our way to follow you in all that comes our way.

WEDNESDAY, APRIL 19, 2000

Early AM at work! I feel good about the day. Last work day of the week is great. I look to it as a peaceful day and truly a day to usher in the 2000 Triduum. Jesus, I present to you – for healing, wholeness, a sense of fullness and self-worth – David, Brian, Lynn and Dwight, Charlotte, Nick, Rose, Ernie & Jan, Sisters and Brothers-in-law, work place persons, especially Kevin. Bless me too! Continue to be energy for me as the day unfolds.

FRIDAY, APRIL 21, 2000

GOOD FRIDAY

The Tre Ora! Silence/Calmness – Introspection! Yet, this time we take was far from this style when the events took place. There was turmoil, yelling, crowds, tension and whatever else an angry gathering at a religious time could be! The article about us being any different than the Palm Sunday folks is a challenge – not a new one – but one that must be grabbed time and again.

Jesus, may I recognize my crowd side and embrace anew the response to be you!

TUESDAY, MAY 9, 2000

Early AM! I'm getting in the groove to carry on in the discipline. I get excited by a day as today – our director's meeting. It is the coming together – our sense of oneness and focus on a common ground. Bless the time together – may it be valuable for our ministry.

Jesus may yesterday's test show no issues! May this road-bump be a caution for me to continue my health watch – it's going to be life-long.

SUNDAY, MAY 14, 2000

Yesterday turned out to be a blessing and healing day in a most unexpected fashion. Brian calls to say he is coming over. That, and the conversation we had at night, even though filled with his issues, was very fulfilling and redeeming for us all. Brian is Brian is Brian. A glimmer of hope! Jesus may the rainbow shine, even as the storm comes and goes. May it both be remembered and anticipated as we move through the moments of our journey. Give Char, hope and peace. Give her clearing lungs -- remove her infections and any limitations they present to her. Bless this Day!

MONDAY, MAY 15, 2000

Well, Mother's Day was really that. We all (5) sat down at the table to eat. No big fanfare, but very significant in the light of all else. First time since Christmas – Brian Is moving on! Storing some things here. David became calmer – more obvious that drugs are wearing off! May it all continue. Jesus, you are at work. Thank You. Keep trimming!

THURSDAY, MAY 18, 2000

I was just thinking – how rarely I sit and write here of good things, positive thoughts and happy moments.

Again, I come to these pages with wonderment as to why us – more, why Char with this terrible back-side pain – spasms!? Not a day goes by that she doesn't endure some pain – how strong she is! Jesus, touch that back – heal what is happening within her. Give her the strength to cope with it and discover a way to go through it. Lift the other burdens of work, schedules and stress of mind and heart. Bless our day!

WEDNESDAY, MAY 31, 2000

A day to move – Char and I are going to Flagstaff for the day -- to visit the Marriage Minister Certification Session. I look forward to it as an enriching time together. At least it will be a time away from home and heat.

May the beauty of the mountains, the green and the freshness touch our hearts.

I'm reading through my journal. One day, week, month follows the next. The Engagement Experience jumps up from the page accenting a period of the year.

In September, I attended the Diocesan Directors meeting in Texas. I was more interested in the evolution of this group as each year passed. This was the third gathering attended.

After a week away, I was exhausted from the travel, the level of concentration I devoted to the meeting, and the realization that I needed to return to work right away. Sr. Dolorette's birthday was celebrated with an early morning breakfast out! I ate very carefully, but I remained uncomfortable well after returning to the office. I spoke with Sr. Dolorette and her secretary about my condition. They encouraged me to call 911. At issue was the constant pressure in my chest. A second heart attack? I called Char and she decided to have David drive her to the Diocesan Center. By herself, she would get lost.

The firemen arrive and had to deal with me up on the second floor without an elevator. I quickly became the center of attention for all in the building. Char and David arrived just to see me carried down the stairs and out of the building. Sr. Dolorette met David and, later, told me how bothered he was at seeing his dad carried away in this fashion.

At the hospital, I was quickly tested and treated with heart meds. They ruled out the likelihood of this being a heart issue. As the day progressed the attending doctor admitted me but estimated that I had some gastro problem. Char stayed with me through the night. Early the next morning, I was told that I am released to go home, take an anti-heartburn pill and see a gastro Doctor for further consultation.

The year 2000 ended on a disappointing, challenging and tearful note. Lynn and Dwight broke off their engagement for some deeply personal reasons. Their wedding had been set for the spring of 2001, and Char and Lynn had already chosen and purchased a brides' dress. Lynn was sure that problems would get solved and that eventually, she and Dwight would marry in the near future.

Char and I were wise enough to only counsel Lynn if she asked us. Naturally, we assured her that our support and prayers are with her, and reminded her that she was dearly loved by her future in-laws, as well. She spent much time with them discovering Dwight's family history and factors that brought him to this point in his life.

When all issues were resolved and they could see their way clear to look toward marriage once again, Dwight came over to meet with Char and me to, once again, ask our permission to marry our daughter, Lynn. The conversation was brisk and very serious. In the end, we all rejoiced to once again, begin plans for their wedding sometime in 2002. They were overjoyed and we were confident that the Lord's love would prevail in their lives.

The year 2001 turned out to be one of the most eventful years in modern American history. The secular happenings of the day gravely impacted my outlook on life as well as nearly every American's. What's more, what about moving forward in the wake of everything? What do I do in these grave times?

Once again, I took a leave from my journal writing and today, the specific events in our family life and how I felt in the face of them was lost from my memory as well as the printed page.

The occurrence that would become known as 911 placed our country face to face with the evil of hatred – we are attacked! In New York City, Washington, D.C., and a country side in SW PA., defined the physical damage done to us while, at the same time began a period of spiritual suffering as a nation. War appeared to become the answer as we navigated the road to solutions. Nineteen years later, we are still on this road. This date becomes one of those that we remember our spot, exact time, and exact place, at the time of the actions and when we heard of the attack.

I was driving to a Director's meeting at Kino Institute! I called Charlotte at home. She was in tears, begging me to come home because we did not know what would be the next targeted city. After a short, rather distracted meeting, I did return home. More than 3,000 people laid down their lives that day. In retrospect, my impression is we have never been the same as a nation since!

Chapter Thirteen

That Which Never Ends

The page of the new year is turned, and we begin 2002. October 19 is set aside as the wedding day for Lynn and Dwight. As parents of the bride, Char and I (especially Char and Lynn) place our lives in overdrive. What needs to be done, who is taking care of this and that, and, what is to be the expense of such celebrating? Gradually, and with firm determination, lists are made, family assignments given, and checks are made next to the items. I could not believe how fast the time went and how long the lists continued to grow.

I never stopped being amazed at the calmness, practical planning and spiritual substance Lynn and Dwight displayed over the weeks and days prior to their wedding. They counseled with Fr. Dennis, St. Benedict pastor, chose scripture readings, selected hymns and music, and signed off for me to offer comments at the marriage Mass. How honored I felt! Char coordinated the reception and dinner event of the day. To her surprise, she gathered friends and others to share their know-how in such matters. Her abilities at leading a team proved to be very important and, in the end, provided a splendid evening.

When I did my first measure for a tux in mid-August, I decided that I must lose some weight. I started Weight Watchers on September 1. By the time I went to pick up the tux, about a week before the wedding I came down one full suit size. I had lost about nine pounds.

For Char and me, the marriage day was truly a family day. Relatives from near and far gathered with co-workers, friends, young and old, as well as our ministry partners. I savored the opportunity to briefly preach about the sacredness of marriage.

I spoke using the scripture verse:

"And what does the Lord require of you, but to Do justly, to love mercy, and to walk humbly with your God."

--Micah 6:8

The day ended with a reception of dinner, dance well-wishes, and the traditional sending forth of the bride and groom on their honeymoon.

On the 28th anniversary of our marriage, Nov. 7, instead of usual dinner out, Char and I spent the night together at the hospital. I had my second heart attack! Fortunately, it was classified as minor.

Such is how 2002 leveled off and ended.

My journal notes will become the telling of this new year unfolding. Here I share of events, my reactions, family, sensitivities, and the on-going blend of Char's and my life.

As I now read the pages, it is a journal of a soul!

WEDNESDAY, JANUARY 1, 2003

A year of trust/hope/loving care! I wish to live, think, speak with NO FEAR – to not move about with a pall over me.

The "darknesses" of health, government, church, war, misdoings, worries, and other's and my own action and inaction is shadowed by His Presence in and around me. The reading, walking, relation moments all contribute to being well and embracing Faith in Jesus. The natural "Think Positive", becomes supernatural grace!

THURSDAY, JANUARY 2, 2003

Back to work! There is some excitement, some apprehension. What lies ahead! But I need to be positive. I'll write more after I'm there awhile. It's after lunch – rather slow morning. Peter's breakfast was a good time. Char's love note was a real picker-upper! I look forward to walking later. Inspired by Peter's stories in his life! Maybe I'll revisit the book idea!!!

FRIDAY, JANUARY 3, 1993

Lord, I equate with Self! Midmorning: Walking is done and my meeting is done. That was an experience of deep faithfulness – the Philippines, ME, another culture – another approach. I have a sense of positive energy today. Maybe it's the decision to work at home on Monday. I made my time a simpler time.

The Gospel today of John the Baptist accents for me the "Let God/Let Go" that is part of the life I live. I pray for David!

SUNDAY, JANUARY 5, 2003

A new insight – the welcoming of the stranger! How often this presents itself – the waitress – the clerk – the people across from me eating – from another culture of the world/France, I think! Do all speak to me of God? But, then, I must ask – do the folks of my life speak to me of God – David, Brian, Lynn, Dwight and especially Char? Do I listen. These are to be Epiphanies on a regular, daily basis and both situations have their challenges!

Taking this morning slowness – even in a restaurant – is valuable. I look ahead to Len. To Char and I being together – taking time. May the Love here shine, be strong, and be You, Jesus, for both of us. Help me to be Positive!

MONDAY, JANUARY 6, 2003

It's closing out the afternoon. I've moved about a lot, did some work, and had a day to myself in great measure. The fighting of worry is constantly with me; it's a major stressor. The relaxation exercise time is a real plus! I realize that I'm distant from David, but I am always concerned about him, in all ways! Char's drug observations and insights haunt me. Do we need to cut him loose when this car thing is complete? Jesus, keep him safe, whole, simple and sacred!

TUESDAY, JANUARY 7, 2003

In the middle of the day! Early rise and in the office before 7:10!

Energy is wearing down at this noon time. The thought of getting out and away keeps coming forth. Another place, different challenges, more people – face to face contact is needed. Will the new building bring this? Do circumstantial changes make a difference? Hearing appointment! Help? Aging!!

WEDNESDAY, JANUARY 8, 2003

It's late today – 7:45 PM. It's the second day with no relaxing time. Why? Things crowded in – but that's the point! This needs to be set as a <u>real</u> priority--time, space, calmness and refreshment. The things can slide in so easily. Morning is key to all this.

THURSDAY, JANUARY 9, 2003

It's after I am home from the conference and all afternoon, David has haunted me. I did give him choices and he is planning to move out! Now! I'm glad I did the talking. I was geared up to do something "large" after the very long day. I'm a part of a foreign group that is very hard for me to relate with. Hopefully tomorrow has more relevant content to it.

FRIDAY, JANUARY 10, 2003

Early morning. So many emotions have come forward about David--his leaving, his life, his goals, his maturity, etc. I want to bottle them up and move on. For me, it is not good to dwell– worry is bad – to become stressed is the worst. I felt good about our conversation that brought this all to a head. It's the actual part of him leaving that did me in. I'm glad it isn't foggy again. There is clarity – light! Let it be in me, in Char, and in David. Jesus, may we see the Light – not Darkness as each day unfolds.

I pray that there is a part in this conference for me!

SATURDAY, JANUARY 11, 2003

It's 3 PM – a long day. Men's meeting – it was disappointing. We got nowhere with just three of us. At least I relaxed and did some Christmas clean-up! Dave just came in – I place him in your hands. I pray for his change of heart – a conversion! Hopefully the rest of the day will be a good pace – movie, etc.

SUNDAY, JANUARY 12, 2003

It's late Monday afternoon. I forgot all about writing yesterday. I even forgot my relaxing time. Enough with the beat-up time.

I just viewed a beautiful reflection that Dolorette sent – God Cares! I go back to the "He holds me in the palm of His hand." I am so worried about Char.

Her breathing is so labored. Jesus – take away the drainage so that she becomes healthy.

I prize her, I miss her excitement, vitality, and her get with-it-ness. Not in a selfish way, but in such a bond together way. We've become the "this and that," the Ying/the Yang, the inside and out. Don't let me think negatively! As the meditation said, we grow old and desire to be young. "To be in the place where I am".

MONDAY, JANUARY 13, 2003

As today's reading accents, "You know me!" May I accept the blessings, graces, people position, possessions, duties, privileges, etc. that are gifts for me. I need to renew each day--in its own right as the most important time for me to be! Bless David in his wanderings and wonderings and may he do what he needs to do to be David at his best.

TUESDAY, JANUARY 14, 2003

Again, the end of the day! I so don't want to just fit – or merely to squeeze it in. Today I am overjoyed by Murphy's call to be regular help with Engaged Encounter. I interview with priests to talk at Synod. Idea! Miriam, the Family Life Office secretary, can do the hospitality in AM at training. And, weight loss – 2.4 more pounds, so not much to go.

WEDNESDAY, JANAURY 15, 2003

Early AM! Expectations for the day: As always should be, is to hear and respond to the Lord's call; meet with the Murphy's; get to the party (baking) for Miriam; get on the conference call about the refugee issues; and the Family Journey. For me, to be about so many things – the most important--is to do Your Will, Lord. Allow me the eyes and ears today to experience You in all these matters and bless Char to improve her lungs without prednisone.

THURSDAY, JANUARY 16, 2003

How wonderful it was to have the AM reading match the session theme – God's mysterious call to us! I enter today with the prospect of meeting with new people and new approach! The Board will walk with me in the EE journey! Exciting.

FRIDAY, JANUARY 17, 2003

I'm tired this AM. The trip to work seemed long, but not really. Yesterday was a blessing – interest and involvement seem to be present. I find myself keeping before me my limitations/need to care for myself. I'm very conscious to not overextend myself. With all of this, work is a burden – I'm tired of it. Yet, the reality is that there may be many years of it ahead. How shall I cope? One thought – One day at a time. A long weekend!

SATURDAY, JANAURY 18, 2003

In all that transpires you are with me! It is so good to do this relaxation thing. There are so many things to do, to get at, to consume my energy and spirit, pacing is important. This week has been a call – a choice – recognizing – following – commitment – confidence and presence. Certain things are more important than others. The choice is always here to take the better part.

MONDAY, JANUARY 20, 2003

The task is to be stable, unstressed and striving to grow. One thought I had while driving to appt. was that I should respond each day to a question. What encouraging or blessing factors touched my life yesterday, today? This will prompt me to reflect a little and not feel driven to write! We'll go for it tomorrow.

WEDNESDAY, JANUARY 22, 2003

Late in the day! Today's resources – a soft walk in the field of work; good walk on the streets of the neighborhood; very light eating; easy-going home time! In pops Brian and all goes up – tempo! Tomorrow will be hard news for Miriam. Work is a drag until I get going with a program. I thought of Len more today – he has such a load to carry! I need to take some time to determine how to be more for him memories – our lighter side.

SUNDAY, JANUARY 26, 2003

*Yesterday was such a long and involved day!
Being present to all sorts of people is the joy I embrace
and the grace that I experienced. The tiredness at the end
broke me some – got out of "sorts" and needed sleep. The
creep of worry about my legs comes to me then.*

*The loss of confidence! Today is another bright,
sun-shiny day of strength, vitality, some new ventures and
time for Char and me to be together. You embrace us. We
celebrate today with Mary and Greg.*

*May that be a "freeing", "relaxing" time.
Blessings and Peace and Hope growing for Brian, Lynn
and David. May David not lose track!*

MONDAY, JANAURY 27, 2003

*How hard and over-bearing yesterday became
with David roaring through to tell his story of being
robbed. David, I love you and care about you. I'm sorry
about the bad and hard things that happen to you. I wish I
could protect you from them, but, I can't. That's what
growing up and older means. I so want you to be healthy
in mind, spirit and body. I believe that will only happen as
you escape from the grasp of "pot". It is so plainly a
limitation to you. Somehow, someplace, you'll get the
picture – and be free to be the mature, sensitive and
caring person you were created by God to be.*

SATURDAY, FEBRUARY 1, 2003

Well, the long day begins! Already I've done some things and it's 8 am. May take each time period as significant moments of grace to receive and to give. Bless the Mass speaking for the Annual Bishop's Appeal.

SUNDAY, FEBRUARY 2, 2003

David holds in my mind with his poor judgment and misplaced outbursts. The cutting is hard, but necessary!

I can't forget Len! How privileged I feel as I go about my "stuff". He can't. Let him never be out of my living!

Chapter Fourteen

Our Family's Tragedy

It's Tuesday, March 18, 2003, and the sun is shining. I feel more positive today. I am praying I may walk into what is mine to do. There are challenges, but I realize that I am specifically gifted to meet them. How I wish I did not feel burdened by my work and that the elements of ministry would clearly spring out and present themselves to me.

THURSDAY, MARCH 20, 2003

It is Thursday morning. Two days, ago, the Tuesday nights' tragic killing of our son Brian will become part of the fabric of our lives. Few happenings, persons or things achieve this. But, even at this early reaction point, I know this will be the case. I know too, that, after this initial time we will all be better if we seek support, counsel, and a listening ear. The loss of life in a family circle is terrible, knowing, yet challenging, cause for good and grace. There is expansion that is necessary – beyond our house doors to welcome friends, others to hold us and for us to hold. May the moments of hugs and tears be blessing points in this day. May Brian be at Peace!

Char and I came home from work about 5:30 PM. That was the first surprise. We commented to each other about Brian and what he wanted from us!

He was staying at our home for several weeks waiting for his younger brother to be ready to rent an apartment together. Brian has a new job and David was going to start working again at a woodworking shop. Perhaps then, our house will be our own.

Back to the surprises! Brian made dinner for us – his treat. He had gathered some cooking interest in his years working at <u>Mi Amigos</u>, a Mexican grill in and around Phoenix. I'll come back to his work there a little later in the story. The dinner conversation was delightful. Brian had matured a great deal in the past few years. He became good friends with Michael, a young man who had moved to Arizona from Boston. Michael was a practicing attorney in Boston but needed to take the Bar exam here before being able to seek a position as a lawyer. He and his fiancé, Allison, planned to marry back east in August. Brian fast became Mike's encourager and guide to all things in and around Phoenix and the East Valley. The four had met because Brian's girlfriend, Laura, and Allison were life-long friends.

Brian took care of the after-meal clean-up duties. He announced that he was staying in tonight and had to get to work rather early the next morning. He said he would watch TV with us if one of the choices was <u>Smallville</u>. We agreed and announced <u>Judging Amy</u> as our choice. All agreed! As <u>Smallville</u> ended, we talked a little about his new job. Brian was excited to be part of the crew that went out of town to install at agencies and companies around the state. Then, <u>Judging Amy</u>, began and we settled in to help Brian to follow the show's story line.

At the first commercial, Brian announced that he was going outside to have a cigarette and to call Michael to see how his studying was doing.

We heard a bang and both Char and I got up to see what the strange sound was. Brian burst into the house and collapsed on the laundry room floor. He shouted that the kid next door shot him.

"Where?" I asked.

Brian showed me his back. I laid Brian on his stomach to keep the blood inside. Urging him to show me that he was conscious, I asked him to talk to me. Brian came in and out of speaking to me.

All this time, Char was in the garage with 911, explaining what she knew to have happened. By the time she was finished, police vehicles were all over the street and officers were coming into the house. Throughout these fleeting moments, I stepped fully into my parent role and out of priesthood, failing to ask Brian if he wished to confess anything and have me give him the Last Rites. This fact haunted me for months to come.

The paramedics had Brian secured on a gurney. Char and I stood about 15 feet from him, calling out our deepest expressions of love to him, telling him he will be OK.

The commotion and noise in our little house continued to increase! The police detective introduced himself and expressed his heart-felt sympathy to Char and me. He then began to ask us question after question about the time-line of the evening. We explained that Brian had identified the young man next door as the shooter.

Brian was being prepared to be taken by ambulance to a wide-open intersection near-by where he would be air-lifted to Scottsdale-Osborn Trauma Center for surgery. Lynn drove the half-hour drive to us and joined us at home. Her husband, Dwight was working in Flagstaff, AZ, and despite that he and Brian were very close, could not be there. Lynn would accompany Char and me, along with the police victim advocate on the way to the trauma hospital.

The detective explained that our house had become a crime scene and that we will be taken to a hotel for the night after we finished at the hospital. The noisy, whirlwind of activity grew nearly silent as two young women drove us to Scottsdale. They were very kind and gentle to us and we found their knowledge and explanation of what will be happening very helpful.

At the hospital, we went into the waiting room just inside the entrance. Two doctors came to us and shared the procedures they were about to do to stop the bleeding and repair several organs damaged by the bullets. Within fifteen minutes a nurse came and escorted us to a more private room where we were joined by Dwight's parents, Brian's friend, Michael, and his brother, John. Several of Brian's other friends were on hand as well.

Within a few minutes another doctor came to us and asked Char and me to step out into the hall. He explained to us that he was the lead surgeon helping Brian. And then, very simply and without fanfare, he shared with us that Brian had died. He had bled too much and was not breathing during the flight from home.

Our world stopped turning at that moment. My emotions were wild. A sea of questions bombarded my brain at once. Char and I embraced. We grabbed Lynn to join our moment of family love.

We went back into the waiting room and I announced what we were just told. The reaction in the room was of terrible shock and horrific anger at the murderer! Dwight had not yet arrived at that point, and when he did, he shouted his feelings in uncontrolled fashion. Lynn eased his anger, helping him calm down, and then helped him to accept what had happened. Dwight was then able to speak more calmly to the others in the room.

A nurse came to Char and me, and invited us to see Brian's body in a separate room. She said this would be a special consideration for those who wished to join us. By this time, Fr. Pat, who was called by the parish administrator of St. Benedict Church, came to pray with us. Only about five or six of us chose to see him with us. Fr. Pat has a very special gift as a calming presence at a time like this. The prayers Fr. Pat said, might have been from a book, yet he was consoling and enriching as he offered them.

It was about 1:00 AM when we departed the hospital. The police officer asked Char and me where he could pick us up in a couple of hours to take us to a hotel for the night to get a little rest. We went to Dwight's parents' home, and Lynn and Dwight traveled home. Detective Gary picked up our medication and some clothes at the house and then came to take us near Chandler Mall where there are several hotels. Gary found a place after three attempts as it was near the close of winter-visitor season. Later, around 8:30 am, he said he would be back to pick us up to take us home to formally interview us about the night before. The entire experience felt like we were living in a TV crime show. The Desk Clerk awakened us about 7:00 AM and I grabbed a breakfast pastry in the lobby and took one to Char in the room. At about 8:15 am, Gary showed up and took us home.

During our drive, he told us about the kid next door and his story of the events of last night. The young man was having a hard time accepting that he had killed Brian. He was arrested on First Degree murder charges.

After a horrific 24 hours, we awoke in our home. There were two things notable about yesterday. First, seeing Brian before the mortician did his work was a very good – holy experience. Touching him and kissing him was very healing. Then, finally, it was a blessing when David got home from Mexico three days later. He showed up about 12:30 AM and despite being tired, he handled the news reasonably, and ended up staying at home with us. It had been a busy morning – there were no signs that it would lessen as the day moved along. I'm feeling a little on edge and burdened. I prayed that peace be with us. As Saturday turned into Sunday and I began to prepare for Brian's funeral on Monday. I made notes, read material to Brian and from Brian, and felt prepared.

Throughout these days before the funeral, a steady stream of young people, friends and acquaintances of Brian's, co-workers and parish friends of Char's, and ministry people from St. Benedict passed in and out to help discuss funeral plans and celebration needs. Char and I went to the cemetery to select a burial plot, a tombstone, and an urn. These matters are small in fashion, but they are all very significant as they celebrate the meaning and value of a young man – our Brian.

The phone rang continuously, or at least it seemed to. The word seemed to circulate so quickly!

I received a call from Bishop O'Brien that was one of the most consoling to me, not because he was bishop, but because he was very tender in his words and so reflective in the thoughts he offered to Char and me. I found working for him during this time to be such a grace.

A couple of Char's catechists took over the phoning of our family and friends to share the news of Brian's death and of funeral details. We were never short of food, refreshments and snacks at the house thanks to their calls.

As I reflect on this week, I am more convinced that it was a pivotal juncture of our family's life. After this week, I watched as our sense of family became graced with a new freedom within each, individually, to seek new roads, and to expand God-given gifts. More on this insight later. And then, the day before Char and I were set to bury our son, on the anniversary of my Dad's death. It's humbling, how life unfolds and then, folds back up. Tomorrow, I will speak of the youth of adventure, excitement, strength, and constant striving. What a blessing to having found an insightful article from 1979. Even now, Brian is still teaching!

The atmosphere was a little hyper in preparation for Brian's Funeral Mass! I look ahead to some calm time and moments of free reflection--that would not be today!

The "public push" of a family death is very draining, emotionally, and physically. There was such a strong strength of community around us and the few testimonies offered were extraordinarily touching for us. Especially significant were David's thoughts and words. Brian be with us today!

The Funeral Mass was a beautifully celebrated expression of a community's belief in the Lord's on-going work of grace in one person's life as well as His assurance to all of life everlasting in God's gracious arms. The Church was filled with the whole spectrum of faithful, from children, youth, and young adults, to middle aged and seniors. We were a community of clergy, religious-vowed women, parents and those of all faith practices. "Holy God we praise thy Name!" Has Brian become a spark of hope to such a wide and diverse assembly? I say, Yes, he has!

Our community was made up of friends from Yuma and longtime friends from North Canton. Jim and Joanne were our best friends there and had been present for Char and me in our early parenting days with Brian.

On the other side, we were surprised to learn that my brother Ernie and his wife, Jan, could not come. Several others who were close to us in Yuma also were unable to be there.

We marked this as an unforgettable time of our lives. To speak yesterday was so special as the outpouring of so many was the strength of the day! Gathering after with Fr. Richard, the young people, and the Browns was a blessing. I was struck while walking, realizing I did not invite Brian to confess and absolve him – parenthood rose over priesthood. I look now to Brian to be our strength.

Next Steps

Moving forward from this, I tried not to push myself as I realize the ongoing issue will be our strength--our ability to go on. The meaning of grace comes to me – free, unrestricted, and unconditional, God's direct revelation to us. My prayers turn to holding on to this and being able to preach this.

Tears will come and go, feelings will slow and hasten, but, being and doing for others as the Lord will have us, as Brian fully knows now, is what is key!

Char and I talked over our immediate future and decided that the best therapy would be to return to work. We knew that there, we could find communities that care about us. We will be asked how we are doing, and we would be allowed to answer the question.

Many fellow staff persons, in both offices are persons of faith as well as loving, caring persons. Yet, as we got into the swing of things, it was clear by words, body language, and facial expressions, that anyone outside of our immediate circle of co-workers, were uncomfortable. Interacting with us was a strain and they viewed us as a mystery.

"How can he/she do it?"

During April – June 2003, the Church was deeply embedded in the Priest Sexual Abuse Scandal. Stemming from an east coast issue, many dioceses and priest/bishops across the United States became highlighted by the spotlight. Within the Diocese of Phoenix, issues and priests surfaced as perpetrators of the abuse. Very popular priests found their ministry ended by removal from assignments, and were sanctioned and were returned to the lay state.

Bishop O'Brien was involved in the scandal, somehow. I don't recall any of it but I do remember what brought about his down-fall. It all came because of an accident that happened as he was driving home after an evening Confirmation ceremony at a parish. A man stepped out in front of the Bishop's moving car, rolled over the hood, broke the windshield, and fell into the road. Bishop thought the interaction was a bird and kept driving.

He was arrested the next day because he failed to stop. Orders from Rome immediately relieved Bishop O'Brien of his position as Bishop of Phoenix. This was a bad situation that immediately became worse, way worse! Bishop was sentenced to 5 years' probation and hundreds of hours of community service.

The Archbishop of Santa Fe, New Mexico became pro-tem Bishop of Phoenix. All of this launched a year-long change in the movement of the diocese as far more conservative thinking began to take over.

It's Easter weekend and I reflect on this time. Love outlasts death. Light overcomes darkness. In Death, we learn Life is not ended, but merely changed. It's today's truth as we read of evil, the strength of control, and the terribleness of violence leading to death. We have lived this during Lent – yet the rainbow of life touching life consecrates all! Will there always be Good Fridays? For simple people, for innocent persons? Yes! Will they lead to resurrection? Absolutely! Brian, be our instrument of Faith.

On Easter Sunday, I'm reminded that miracles do happen! Stones move. People see and change. Day and night come and go. Yet, in all this, God is constant – a mystery maker as He knows, and He lets us be. We recognize the wonders and greet the change. We welcome the difference. This week is to be different – appointments, packing, celebrating, moving, traveling, being with friends – facing death again. In all of this there will be challenge, joy, peace, hope and your presence. I pray to never separate your presence from the life I live. Brian, you are no longer the immature, unknowing, lacking judgment one. You have the vantage point of being our guide – supporting us and sharing the wisdom we need.

I prayed that our coming together, on Easter, be one of family, community, sharing, and love beyond all telling!

By this time, I was well established as the Director of the Office of Family life. Charlotte carried on at St. Benedict in her remarkably splendid fashion. She would be moving to the new St. John school adjacent to the parish property about two miles away.

Lynn and Dwight continued to settle into their home far away at "Magic Ranch." David wanted to move out of the house very much. He was not able to, mostly because he did not have the money. He floated around various jobs, unable to land on one that he liked.

Again, as has often happened in our lives, Char and I began thinking at the same time about retiring from our jobs! Neither of us had complaints about our work situations, but Brian's death was taking its toll emotionally, and psychologically on us.

An issue arose in Charlottes' work as the parish was sold to another church community. They needed the religious education classrooms immediately. Char needed to move all program supplies and classroom needs to St. John Bosco School. There, she did not have an office. Her session days were filled with moving classroom needs back and forth from the old property. The most annoying thing for Char was that she did not have a building key for the school office--the most revolting situations stem from the simple and small.

Toward the end of April, I traveled to Ohio to visit Len and Barb. He looks good, seems to feel fair – but his breathing taxed and he uses more oxygen that I expected. Emotion, laughter, visits, and exercise filled the days. I experienced one of Len's panic situations. How frightful. One can sense that he is leaving us and the tension was terrifying. With meds, time, and attention he came back around. How limited I felt, much like the times dealing with Char's asthma. Afterwards, Len said to me, "I'm sorry you have to go through this." When I finally connected with Char, it was good, very good talking with her. It is stunning how very limited Len had become! Death is so holy and so terrible; it is what we live for and so, it is also what is greatly feared as we live. As I shared with Char, I found this time to be such a lonely time. Tears washed over Char yesterday – cleansing and healing. Will that come for me? How? When? If? I continue to look to Brian to intercede for me, for us. I prayed for him to be our teacher and guide us to learn life's values and vitality; to live in the tensions of life so that the spiritual will be sensed, treasured, and bring us to your loving and forgiving God.

My best friend in life and in death is Len. We've been close since early high school days and for 47 years, nothing had interfered with our friendship! It was time for us to face the end time. Len had terminal lung cancer. I had been routinely faithful in phoning him weekly on Sunday afternoons. Also, about every two months, I traveled to Cleveland for a three to four-day visit. By early May, Len became nearly bed confined and was told that his life expectancy was only four to six months!

Around the fourth of July in 2003, I paid what would be, my last trip to visit with him. I found him in noticeably worse condition. His Hospice nurse was now coming daily to help him. During this time, I stayed at his mom's home. At 90 years old, she was in amazingly good health. The two of us would stay with Len from morning to evening. Then, on Sunday afternoon, when he and I were alone, he called me over to his bed.

Len looked at me and in his horse-throated voice, he asked that I look after Jake and help him in these young-adult years. I immediately said yes, not really knowing what this would mean for either me or Jake. He and his sister were carrying out their closeness to the church primarily to please Len and Barb, their parents.

Our own children have gone through their own separations from the Catholic Church. Young people leaving the Catholic Church remains one of the great challenges of the church today.

In these days, weeks, months, I realized the value of Mary Z, my counselor, more and more. She has been a valuable guide, listener, and spiritual helper to me.

In less than a week, our family will be attending court. My emotions are so mixed--I am afraid, angry, and anxious as we approach the justice system and among my concerns is that the road will be very long and we will endure it all. I turn to Brian that he may lead us in light, not darkness. Lynn is expecting to interview in a few days to be Char's secretary. I pray she be guided to say what is valuable and that she excels there. I thank the Lord for the family around me and that we all support one another, particularly now. I continue to look to Brian as I believe he is the ringleader for this stage.

Len's progressing illness overwhelms me. I think about how he grows worse and endures maintenance treatment to help remain comfortable. It is so difficult. I think about the book Tuesdays with Maury and I wish I could do the same. I know I do not want to let Len go as he ties together so much of my life: youth, young-adulthood, leaving priestly ministry, marriage, contact from a distance, and now, finally this past year.

Again, I look to Brian to give Len a word of confidence – in that his passage was quick – to be his strength as he moves slowly! Lord, let your love and light shine upon Len, Barbara and his family. Be a guide to me on this path of life!

We made it through the first court session for the young man who shot Brian as he submitted a mental ability plea. Now, our family will wait for evaluations and decisions as everything moves very slowly.

In this months after Brian's death, our family finds comfort together with family dinners a source of care and gratitude. I find myself with tears at times as I wish I knew what Brian had in his mind as he died. What did he think while he was still at home? What did he feel or think on the way to the hospital? Or, when his heart was revived? I wonder, was he able to think, realize, care, feel? I wished so deeply that he could enlighten me. In reflection after, I am touched by how hard it was for me to handle Brian's death and Len's dying. There were too many issues to embrace for me.

The summer continues with a constant series of up and downs.

Chapter Fifteen

Summer of 2003 - The Road to Retirement

It's June 2003. Life continues as Char and I grow accustomed to our lives without Brian. Even every day events like Sunday dinners are enjoyable yet they highlight his absence. Without much warning, a sinking feeling just appears reminding me that Brian will not be "showing up, dropping by", nor will we hear from him. As a physical reality, he is gone. He always had such a special ability, a gift to call out for others, to let-up, let-go, to "be cool", and to "chill out". Life is too short – and it really has been so for him. He didn't do all he wanted, but he always looked ahead. My meetings with my counselor, Mary, continue to be good, healthy, and healing as she reminds me that time has an ongoing healing effect. Lord, please, inspire me to be this way and, Char, may you be lifted up! I continue to pray that Brian will be present to us and continue to bless us.

Life is change and as we grow older, change becomes even more challenging. I learned Russ has one major blockage. As I think about him, realizing he is alone, I think how difficult that would be for me. Changes are certainly in his future, some that will not be so easy. Sometimes, I still fail in eating well and often still struggle managing "stress".

At the Diocese, the bishop situation upsets me. I would quit in a minute if I could. The level of dishonesty that runs through it all is difficult to overlook.

Bishop O'Brien has become a pawn in the hands of lawyers and business types. I cannot help but wonder if this is indicative of the entire church leadership. It's all very discouraging as I continue to find myself in a bad way about all this Church controversy. I blame, I feel sorry for myself, and I constantly am thinking of what to say at various meetings. It is all so wasteful! I must keep finding ways to let go – to separate from it as none of it serves me well. The effort and ease I've had to employ to be calm at work needs to continue. I must never look too far ahead or too deeply into issues and keep doing what I can and be the best I can.

Char emerged from her heavy, downcast period in July just before my trip to visit Len, I was so glad. I love her so and it is so hard to see all the trials and tribulations she endures. It's very tempting to let go. It's time for me to reflect on what possibilities there are for us over the next several years. Thinking about these options raises some excitement in me.

I paid a visit to Len and stayed with his Mom during the visit. I discovered more about myself as I stayed there realizing I am entrenched in my own ways. It's strange staying there as I can see clearly how particular and, even picky, I am. When I made my way to see Len, it was alarming how much weaker he was appearing nothing like he had been last time. Then, as I stumbled on the steps to keep myself from going down, I strained my back muscles. I was embarrassed and felt like the experience detracted from Len. Sore and worried, I hoped I did not do something worse. I then learned that Len had had a hard night; I really did not understand what that meant.

As the days passed, my back improved and I was more relaxed. The moments toward my final visit with Len are ticking by and I am nervous. Will I see him again? How long will he live? What do I say and how? I strive to be faith-filled and know that the Lord's grace is enough for me. I know it will all come, and will likely not be easy or smooth, but I will find the words.

"I'll see you again."

As I said my goodbyes to Len, there was no way to say: "for the last time" yet we did agree on "we'll see". He said that God is in charge and that he wants to keep living! I don't think that he sees his quality of life being lessened – changed, simpler, calmer. These days are good days. Yet now, I can feel the tears are just under the surface.

Then, as the days passed, I think about Len in his ebb and flow of living and how small his window is becoming. I continue to embrace Brian through thoughts, memories, some dialogue and writing. The whole spectrum of living comes to play each day and I need to recognize and rejoice in this reality.

It's been a few weeks since my visit and when I called Len today, sadly, he was in no condition to talk as Death is close for him. I told Char that I have been so close to Len for so long that it's like watching yourself die. Now, it's just waiting for the Call!

It's Monday, July 21, 2003, and I know it all going to be very hard. Len is strong in Faith and Thought, and Physically, and he perseveres! As Barb talked, I wish I could be there with him and maybe do for him what I didn't think of doing with Brian – prayer and Reconciliation. That evening, at 6:45, I learned Len had died at about 5:30. It was a peaceful end. But, just the beginning – no more tears!

Our Cleveland visit for Len's funeral and burial was a splendid celebration of life, so good to experience old friends last night and today. There is a specialness to be in the place where memories were lived! We live an apart life, yet we have carved out our niche! Upon our return, our family gathered for a very slow and enjoyable dinner out with all except Brian. How he loved these things. This evening, we celebrated Birthdays – Char's, Dwight's, and Allison and Mike's wedding coming on Saturday. Many times, I've thought about Len and our weekly phone conversations. All at an end, now. I know I will be calling Jake and Barb, as walking with them and they with us, is very important. Family is valuable! Lord, use Brian and Len, lead me to a valuable path to be with and for David. Please give him insight, strength, and self-realization to move ahead.

Char and I return home for a few days and then we set off for a vacation like we've never gone on before. For two weeks, we are off to the San Diego area to stay in a Native American Hotel on a reservation.

WEDNESDAY, JULY 30, 2003

Evening – it's been a long day – driving, new surroundings, but we are away and moving in the direction of calming down and being slow moving. We look forward to something different each day! As Char was struck at dinner, this is Brian's gift. Thank you, Brian! I guess I've not run into anything that is provocative. The place where we are is so great – clean, sharp, and well-presented. It feels good being here. Sadly,

Dwight's mom is not good! Brian be with your friend as he goes through this with his mom.

THURSDAY, JULY 31, 2003

Morning – a good day start! Walk, exercise, shower, shave. Plan to go to San Diego for trolley trip and see what else there is to see and do! I feel relaxed. This is what this is about, losing the tension! We walk in hope that this is a for taste of the life of retirement and more, the life of heaven. The picture on the wall says that wild land has been changed into modern use for pleasure, the old gives way to the new!

TUESDAY, AUGUST 5, 2003

We had a most calm, peaceful, fresh time at the beach – watching the sun journey to its disappearance "into the ocean". Stunning. I did some poor driving moves that soured our going there! Always something to work on! Always thought of Brian! Char and I had a great, exciting, interlude before we had our brunch. Now, today, we're off to Sea World! Hopefully not too exhausting.

THURSDAY, AUGUST 7, 2003

Our cruise was wonderful. So many extraordinary happenings! Water, sunset, dinner, dancing, and lights-- all a gentle reminder of the life that is ours. I think of Len – his interests in so many things. How I wish we could have done more together. The same applies to Brian – yet he is family and we did what we could when we could. Today we see the ocean life center. I hope it is fantastic!

We celebrate Char's birthday with a movie and an Indian festival. Lynn called. Dwight is traveling again and it's very hard on her. She is learning that it may be a long-term thing and even harder, there is a prospect of Lynn and Dwight moving, too. This would be hard on both families, but especially for Char.

WEDNESDAY, AUGUST 13, 2003

Well, the end is here! How good this trip has been! There have been a lot of variety and a good deal of easy-going days. It will be hard to hit the heat again. And, it will be even harder to hit the realities of life-home and work. Tomorrow will be tense as the court situation is before us. I tend to want to make resolutions and look at return as a new beginning for fresh starts. But, really, I should be grateful for what has been and just enjoy the slow down mode as it lingers on. There are no killer issues in that area. I'll have to pay some price – maybe real money -- and work at weight for a while. Lord, keep us safe for driving and may all be well! Brian and Len!

With vacation days at an end, Char and I enter, once again into our work lives, the start-up of the activity time of the year. Programs, plans, and preparation go into high gear. Char's use of the St. John Bosco school is further complicated due to a change of the secretary and a cut-back of her work time to save on the budget.

There was no letting up on this position by the administration or Fr. Dennis. For my part, after five years of the Engagement Experience in one style, I was very hopeful that some refreshing elements blend into this valuable experience for engaged couples.

Not so long after our vacation, Char and I began to have long conversations and some sincere prayer time concerning our work lives. Brian's death is beginning to settle upon us. We are only 62 years old, but we have both aged a lot in the past couple of years. Char's multiple program times requires that she be outdoors in the late afternoon and evening times and her asthma is becoming a greater issue. This factor, the lack of a full-time secretary, and the overall feeling of not being supported by the pastor brought her to dig deeper into the reality that it is time to retire. What a hard thought! I wonder, could it be merely an interest in a change of pace? I, too, am looking for that.

Months pass through to Thanksgiving and Char decides firmly to leave ministry and retire. She realizes that there will be a gap at St. Benedict that only she can fill. There will be a lack of her self-giving personality ever responding to the needs of others and her keen sense of organization. Char's last day at St. Benedict was the day before Thanksgiving!

During this time frame of October and November, I spoke with Sr. Dolorette and told her of my need to take some time off due to the personal pressures I am experiencing. I told her of Char's decision and her personal health issues. She indicated that the holiday time and early January would be excellent for such a leave of absence.

The diocese was undergoing great change in that we are assigned a new Bishop coming from out of state.

As was anticipated, he is more conservative and much more of a take-charge person. His background includes nine years working in Rome as an English-speaking assistant to Pope John Paul II.

I began my time away from work in mid-December and planned to be away for about six weeks. I called Jake and Barb to check in and the day took on a special deep awesomeness. Barb is working through Len's death with such emotion and overwhelm; it truly was an extraordinary and beautiful experience. The emotional impact of that call with them lingered with me for days.

Taking a leave from work during the holiday time of the year is a real decision of foolishness. The work issues have gone away, but during this time of year, the schedule for everyone is run, run, run and I am a little stressed for me, and also worries about Char's insurance. I continue to focus on relaxation, reminding myself that NOTHING is as important as my well-being. Thanks to Dwight and Lynn, they are such a blessing. They took care of putting our tree up, and some other "fixes" in the house.

Christmas 2003 was the best of times and the worst of times. The treat of those closest to us was a significant part of Christmas Eve and Day. I really allowed myself to be emotionally involved in cooking, deadlines, how things turn out, and the appearance of everything. Yet, who was it all for, really? We are family! I know I was in a bad way because I was so relieved when we started eating. Too much eating! I gained five pounds from Wednesday to today! The discipline of it all. Good conversation with Jake – he sure is moving ahead.

As the page turns to 2004, I will retire on June 20. My leave ends on February 11 leaving me with about four months to work.

Another segment of our lives begins to unfold! In January, I have an MRI and schedule a meeting with Sr. Dolorette to share my plans. I am nervous about both as the fanfare of returning to work gets to me.

Sr. Dolorette and her secretary treated me to lunch. She passed on the expectations the Bishop had for the Family Life Office before I retire. I knew Bishop had high expectations and I wondered about my ability to meet them. I was upset with the whole session on several levels. The Bishop never approached me personally about his views. He asked for a job description for at least a years' worth of work. As it turned out, my immediate successor resigned after 6 months and the person who has done a splendid job for the past 13 years took a good year or more to settle into his position. And so, I set upon my final time as a Church employee.

The end is here! Rather, I should write that the next phase of my life is to begin. There is no question that I am different in views, values, sense of responsibility.

Now, I want to be more independent, and less the "no contest" good boy. I still value ministry, but not in the context of heavy administration. As I go back to work, I fear the demands, the sense of fast-pace and the "bottom-line" of heavy content-oriented sort of ministry. With each week, it seems, comes Sr. Dolorette dropping by with additional tasks levied on me and the department from the Bishop. As each new task arrives, I find myself experiencing the results of decisions made without any personal contact between he and I. I feel less and less at harmony with him in my ministry. Yet, as the weeks go by and I realize that the tasks are being accomplished, I become more relaxed.

Gradually Char and I solidify our post-employment venture. We are establishing a non-profit corporation to enable us to be parish consultants for advice concerning faith renewal and community spiritual growth.

As I spoke about this, we began to receive various invitations: a weekend retreat for the presenting couples of Retrovaille; a ministry retreat weekend for parish ministers at St. Jerome; a six-week series for leaders of marriage preparation. The key offering that we intend to begin in 2005 is a one-day seminar for engaged couples. We are taking plenty of lead-time for this project because, our hope is to charge the couples a fee! For the seminar to succeed, it needs some level of diocesan endorsement. Sr. Dolorette said that when we get closer to the start date, she will recommend this as an approved program in the diocese of Phoenix.

April arrives and we attend another day at court facing all the emotions that it brings forth. During each one, we relive a portion of March 18th. If there is a full trial, it will be very difficult.

This day at court was painful enough with the remarks from the "other" prosecutor. We learned that we will change attorney's again. I wonder if this will all come together expecting that it probably will not happen without ongoing pain and missteps.

It was April, and Char and I were asked if we intended to move from our house where Brian was murdered. Neighbors were leaving. We never really thought about it. But Dwight and Lynn explained to us that this time was a great time to sell and to buy, especially if we moved out of the central area of the east valley (Chandler and Gilbert). Char and I discussed this weighty decision often over the next several weeks.

In early May, Ayala, who was the mother of the young man who shot Brian, and a neighbor friend of hers came over to visit. This was a surprise to us since more than a year has passed since March, 2003. What started out as a rather cordial conversation turned into a rather accusatory attack at Char and me. She made her son's fate our fault. Char left the room in tears and I ushered them out of the house. Michael got a restraining order to prevent this from happening again.

Later that week, Char answered a real-estate ad in the daily paper about a home available in near-by Mesa. We met with the agent and began to look for a home. We figured that the summer time was ours to accomplish this task. What we failed to realize was that Lynn and Dwight wanted us to live nearer to them!

After a few misfires in seeking the right home for us, dejected, we decided to slowly clean up and fix up our home. I have entered into the final days at the Diocese as Sr. Dolorette advises me to work from home when I can and slow weekend work.

I wonder if it is an act of generosity or a clean way to clear the house so that others may move in more quickly. I discover that I am making terrible judgement calls and I really wish to leave calmly and with a grateful heart.

I then have my answer when Sr. Dolorette stops into my office to tell me that I may stop working in my position after Saturday's EE event. I will be paid until June 30. She tells me that this month is a gift from the diocese for my years of service in the Church. All the paperwork concerning retirement will be handled by the HR department. I will leave Saturday, by myself, from an empty building, with no fanfare. How different! /

Then, in the first week of June, we set out again with our realtor's guidance to see homes that should be much more to our liking and that will fit within our budget. As this effort continues to unfold, it becomes for us an exhausting work that is taking a large toll on all concerned.

Finally, we step forward and put our home on the market. And then a grand announcement: Lynn and Dwight are having a baby! Grandpa and Grandma! *What a joy! Thank you, Lord. "The Peace that was and is meant to be."*

Char and I have a feeling we'll find the right, perfect home we trusted our home would sell quickly. In days, everything happened! We did the deed! Our choice was a beautiful home, yet, it was quite a distance away. And our home sold almost as soon as the day began to the third buyer for full price. Unfortunately, we then learned the home we contracted had five offers to be considered. This meant we were back on the road to look at more homes...

In a summary fashion, Char and I sold our home in Chandler and bought a home in a fast-growing subdivision called Johnson Ranch, about 40 miles southeast of downtown Phoenix. We sign lots and lots of papers that fulfilled the process of selling and buying. We moved into our home with the generous help of many friends, and once again, and we begin to settle into our new life. How much the same the process is, yet each time, there are large scale differences. This time, we are less one family member. Oh, how Brian would have enjoyed this new place.

Conclusion

The priest, the nun, three children, and nine homes in three states! It is the description of Vocation, when God calls, lived to the fullest.

In the fashion of a postscript, some of the outcomes the story told here are that I am 79 years old now. Lynn and Dwight have been married 18 years and are raising three children, Daniel, Jonathan, and Kristin.

David is not married. He is a professional carpenter, specializing in detailed home cabinetry and gaming tables. He drives a nice pick-up truck. His social life has revolved around yoga in a young-adult community and weekend camping with a small group of friends.

Our ministry effort in retirement lasted for 10 years, ending in 2015. It was called CORE. (Community,

Organization, Renewal, Education) Our chief ministry was the preparation of engaged couples for marriage. Over the years, we met with about 3500 couples. Our ministry became a vibrant family affair and even our grandchildren became a part of the hospitality team, helping to serve breakfast, lunch, and snacks.

As I send this off for publication, I share, in grief, Char's death from Stage IV liver cancer on January 13, 2019.

For 10 years, we lived outside metro Phoenix, enjoying our closeness to the grandchildren and the ability to install a beautiful pool in our backyard. We decorated the interior of the master bedroom; it was a hit with visitors from out of town.

The recession in 2008 to 2010 seriously affected our savings and the success of the pre-marriage seminar, CORE. We received a settlement from a wrongful death suit that suddenly dried up as fewer and fewer couples came to the program. All our amenities began to cost more. Finally, at the end of 2013, we decided to downsize our living situation.

In June of 2014, we moved to Mesa, AZ, into a lovely manufactured home park. Char loved our home, but I had trouble with the communal style of living at the park. Much to my surprise, Char was not a joiner here as she always had been in her life. Slowly, I began to figure out that she was in the early stages of Alzheimer's

Disease. Her conversational speed became noticeably limited and so, in early 2015, she didn't want to participate on the seminar team. We decided to drop the program from the schedule of diocesan pre-marriage programs.

As Char's memory continued to fail her, she gave up driving realizing that traffic signs were becoming ever more difficult to follow! In January of 2016, Char's neurologist diagnosed her with Alzheimer's and dementia. By this time, she also was suffering intense abdominal pain and soon after, she had her gallbladder removed.

About this time, Lynn and Dwight began to speak with us about moving in with them. They wanted to move closer to his work offices and would buy a larger home to accommodate us. This took some convincing.

In the summer, we agreed and put our manufactured home on the market for sale. Our home had a lot going for it except interested customers! In July 2017, Lynn and Dwight put their home on the market and set out to look for a newer, larger home. A buyer came forward in two weeks and they worked out a contract. Instantly, they were in high gear to find and buy a home.

As for us, Char's health worsened. Her digestive system continued to cause her more and more discomfort. After a year with the same realtor, and no interest in our home, we changed agents to a woman that had sold a friend's park home in two months' time. She was confident that she could do the same for us. Six months' effort to sell it, she still failed because of illness and some missed appointments combined with her lack of quality sales skills. When her contract ended, I went back to the former realtor. He sat with Dwight and I, offering us only what we still owed on the mortgage. In effect, we made nothing on the home. The grace of all of this was that we lived in a beautiful home with Lynn and Dwight for nearly a year, rent free!

Char continued to fail in health through mid-2018. She lost 25 pounds and finally, just before Thanksgiving, she went again to the emergency room, with a very painful abdomen and was admitted.

The PA who worked on her floor sent her for an MRI. The test was analyzed and we learned she had advanced stage liver cancer. When a biopsy was performed, we were told she had Stage Four, terminal cancer. This was the cause of all her health issues.

Char accepted all this in a very saintly fashion, knowing that this was God's will at work in her life. She was not afraid to die and became a source of encouragement to all of us who lived with her and visited her during the holiday time. She went to three or four doctors who offered treatment options, but she turned them all down. On January 2, 2019, at the suggestion of an oncologist, we decided to contact Hospice of the Valley. A nurse visited the house, evaluated her, and taught me how to administer morphine. After several hours with her, we decided to send her to a Hospice residence home to get the medication orders ironed out.

Char would then return home. At the hospice, she slept most of the time, breathing through her mouth in a very rough fashion. On the third day, the grandchildren and all the family came to visit. She became noticeably excited to see them and sat up to hug each one. This was a real lift for the rest of the family. After everyone left, I got a little container of pudding which I fed to her. She enjoyed it and ate every bit of it to my surprise.

On Monday morning, the house doctor came to see her and checked the nurse's notes. She was a very caring and kind person with a wonderful bedside manner. She was instantly likeable explaining that there was too much irregularity in her morphine need. Her schedule for visiting patients was Monday, Wednesday, and Fridays.

She expressed her doubts that Char would return home. This news was heartbreaking to me. My practice was to come in to her between 7:30 am and 8:15 am. I would kiss her not expecting any reaction from her. I did this on Tuesday and she awoke, opened her eyes, looked at me and puckered her lips as though wanting a kiss again on the lips. This brought joyous tears to my eyes and a spark of hope!

Through the lead nurse, I arranged for a priest to come and give her the Sacrament of the Sick. He came on Wednesday morning with a few women parishioners, in a rather somber fashion, bringing Communion to us. I'm not sure if Char had any realization what was being said and done. When the doctor came, and read Char's chart, she met with me. Her decision was that Char should remain

here. She had only one week, at most, to live. The family-
-especially Lynn, David, and I were sure that Char could
hear us, and perhaps, understand what we spoke. Dave
took up the practice of reading to Mom from spiritual
readings that she loved to read herself.

On Thursday and Friday, several friends of ours
came to visit, notably Susan and Richard from the Home
Park, Pueblo Manor. The four of us became very close to
one another.

Saturday, Jan. 13, started out with my arrival to
her room about 8 am. David came around 10 am while
Lynn and Dwight were at a gymnastic meet with Kristin.
Lynn figured she would be back about noon. Because of
Char's increasingly worsening breathing and her very
poor condition throughout the night, the lead nurse
doubted she would live out the remainder of the day. The
nurse checked on her about every half hour. Finally, at
about noon, she reported that Char was very close to
death and I prayed. The nurse took her pulse and
pronounced her dead at 12:22 pm.

The three of us kissed her as tears came to our
eyes. We stayed in the room a short time more before the
mortuary arrived to pick up her body. During the
following week, all mortuary, cremation, and church
arrangements were carried out. The Funeral Mass was
celebrated with Fr. Charles Parker, my counselor of the
past few years, as the Presider. The Mass was held on
Monday, January 21, at Resurrection parish in Tempe,
AZ, where Char and I led our Engagement Seminars for

10 years. Fr. Charles had been the pastor here before his retirement from active priestly ministry. Char was buried at a family gathering on Friday, January 25. I offered burial prayers and shared some reflections.

Charlotte, RIP, Lord, into Your Hands we commend her Spirit.

Thank you for reading our story!

Richard Bergkessel

Richard Bergkessel

Made in the USA
Monee, IL
04 February 2021